DEDICATED

TO

ELINOR HUGHES

LITTLE LIBRARIAN

The STORY of RELIGION

written and illustrated by

MABLE MANDEVILLE PYNE

1 9 5 4

HOUGHTON MIFFLIN COMPANY BOSTON

The Riverside Press, Cambridge

Long ago, in early ages, the first man struggled to stay alive; by day hunting food, at night cowering in caves— afraid of the dark and afraid of death. After he had invented weapons and tools and created a shelter, he had time to wonder about his world. He saw the sun disappear, but knew it would return the next morning. Plants withered and trees became bare, but he learned that all would be green again, come spring. Men died; he might, himself. Would he live again? That is the mystery.

What happened to the spirit that made a person laugh, eat and run? The American Indian thought it went to the Happy Hunting Ground where huge herds of buffalo roamed, so the dead hunter would surely need his spear and bowl.

The Egyptian thought it best to take everything he owned to the Land of the Dead, and into the tomb went food, clothes, jewels, cooking pots, furniture and his flesh and bones, carefully fixed with oils and chemicals and wrapped round and round with strips of fine linen. The Chinese, too, thought the spirit would need food and clothes and money when it went to join the ancestors, but they buried pictures of the possessions instead of real things.

The Hindu thought the soul was reborn for another life—perhaps better, maybe worse—in a different body. Perhaps, thought others, the spirit lingers, restless and unhappy, in graveyards and old houses. Maybe it floats endlessly in outer space—eternity.

Many still believe the spirit returns home once a year. In India, in China, and in Japan lights are lit, food prepared and the door left open in welcome on a certain night of the year. Until not very long ago this was the custom of the western world—on All Hallow's Eve.

Perhaps there is no future life, think some; all that one does on earth is what counts. Others are sure the soul returns to its Creator.

REST IN PEACE

GODS

Most of the ancient peoples believed that a father god, powerful and wise, watched over them. The Ruler of Heaven and Earth had many names. In China he was the Above-Lord; in Norseland, the Allfather, Odin; in America, the Great Spirit; in Greece, Zeus, the Thunderer; in Italy, Jupiter or Father Jove; in India, Dyaush Pitar, the Sky Father; in Egypt, Osiris, King; in Persia, Mazda, the God of Light, the Lord of Wisdom.

Helping him in the enormous task of overseeing the firmament and the world were gods of wind, rain, fire, sea; of the moon, the rivers, the seasons and the crops. His messengers might be ravens who flew down and reported the doings of men, or the swift god Hermes, also called Mercury, he of the winged heels and winged helmet. Sometimes the great god himself rode down among the mortals, on a white horse, or a white elephant, or in the shape of a white bull.

Often the sun, loved by men for its light and warmth, was said to be the bright good son of the Father Sky God. Homage was paid to many sun gods: fair Baldr, son of Odin, with his shining sun-shaped shield; beautiful Apollo, son of Zeus. American Indians gathered for a solemn sun dance. Chinese Emperors went out, with all the court, to meet the warm spring sun. The Egyptian sun god rode across the skies in a boat.

All this traveling between sky and earth was accomplished with golden slippers, golden chariots, winged slippers, winged helmets, winged horses; Boreas, the god of wind, had wings, Aurora, goddess of dawn, had wings, the Chinese guardian Dogs of Fo had wings. Egypt's Goddess of Truth had wings and the soul of man was pictured as a bird with human face. Angels have wings.

Women, too, had their place in early legends and myths; as the queens of heaven, wives of the Kings; as goddesses of the moon and seeds and growing things; as beautiful servants, the Muses and Valkyries; as the mothers of sun gods. Japanese Emperors were thought to be descended from the Sun goddess; Chinese Emperors were Sons of Heaven. Occasionally these tales tell of the marriage of the Ruler of Heaven to a woman on earth, and of their remarkable offspring, half god, half human.

Despite the gods on high and all men's efforts to be good, terrible things happened—floods, drought, and eclipses of sun and moon. How could one explain misfortune, sorrow and woe? There must be bad gods, too: wicked rulers of evil and darkness—devils.

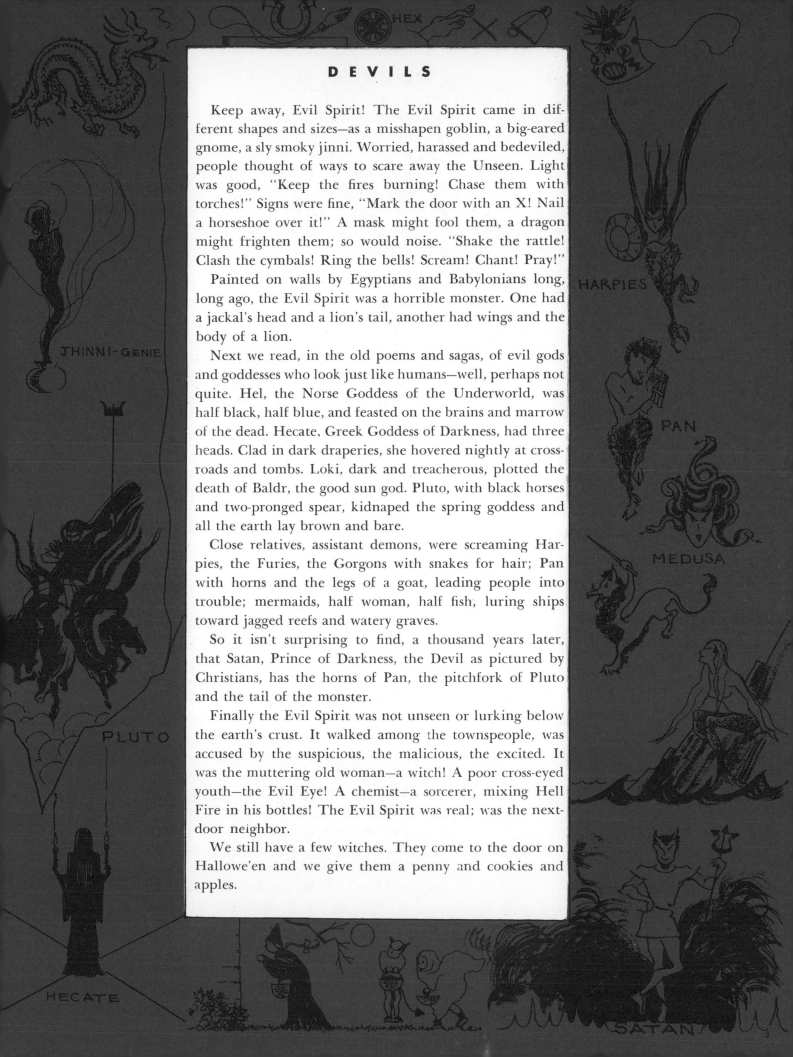

DEVILS

Keep away, Evil Spirit! The Evil Spirit came in different shapes and sizes—as a misshapen goblin, a big-eared gnome, a sly smoky jinni. Worried, harassed and bedeviled, people thought of ways to scare away the Unseen. Light was good, "Keep the fires burning! Chase them with torches!" Signs were fine, "Mark the door with an X! Nail a horseshoe over it!" A mask might fool them, a dragon might frighten them; so would noise. "Shake the rattle! Clash the cymbals! Ring the bells! Scream! Chant! Pray!"

Painted on walls by Egyptians and Babylonians long, long ago, the Evil Spirit was a horrible monster. One had a jackal's head and a lion's tail, another had wings and the body of a lion.

Next we read, in the old poems and sagas, of evil gods and goddesses who look just like humans—well, perhaps not quite. Hel, the Norse Goddess of the Underworld, was half black, half blue, and feasted on the brains and marrow of the dead. Hecate, Greek Goddess of Darkness, had three heads. Clad in dark draperies, she hovered nightly at crossroads and tombs. Loki, dark and treacherous, plotted the death of Baldr, the good sun god. Pluto, with black horses and two-pronged spear, kidnaped the spring goddess and all the earth lay brown and bare.

Close relatives, assistant demons, were screaming Harpies, the Furies, the Gorgons with snakes for hair; Pan with horns and the legs of a goat, leading people into trouble; mermaids, half woman, half fish, luring ships toward jagged reefs and watery graves.

So it isn't surprising to find, a thousand years later, that Satan, Prince of Darkness, the Devil as pictured by Christians, has the horns of Pan, the pitchfork of Pluto and the tail of the monster.

Finally the Evil Spirit was not unseen or lurking below the earth's crust. It walked among the townspeople, was accused by the suspicious, the malicious, the excited. It was the muttering old woman—a witch! A poor cross-eyed youth—the Evil Eye! A chemist—a sorcerer, mixing Hell Fire in his bottles! The Evil Spirit was real; was the next-door neighbor.

We still have a few witches. They come to the door on Hallowe'en and we give them a penny and cookies and apples.

HEX

JHINNI-GENIE

PLUTO

HECATE

HARPIES

PAN

MEDUSA

SATAN

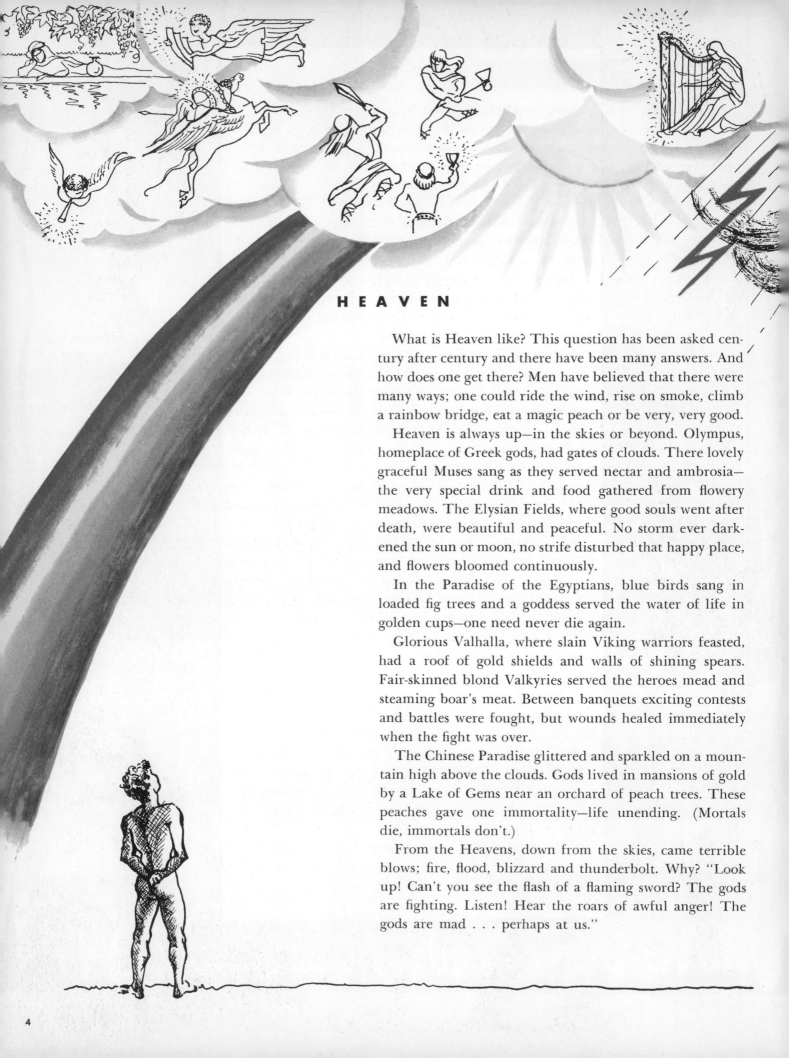

HEAVEN

What is Heaven like? This question has been asked century after century and there have been many answers. And how does one get there? Men have believed that there were many ways; one could ride the wind, rise on smoke, climb a rainbow bridge, eat a magic peach or be very, very good.

Heaven is always up—in the skies or beyond. Olympus, homeplace of Greek gods, had gates of clouds. There lovely graceful Muses sang as they served nectar and ambrosia— the very special drink and food gathered from flowery meadows. The Elysian Fields, where good souls went after death, were beautiful and peaceful. No storm ever darkened the sun or moon, no strife disturbed that happy place, and flowers bloomed continuously.

In the Paradise of the Egyptians, blue birds sang in loaded fig trees and a goddess served the water of life in golden cups—one need never die again.

Glorious Valhalla, where slain Viking warriors feasted, had a roof of gold shields and walls of shining spears. Fair-skinned blond Valkyries served the heroes mead and steaming boar's meat. Between banquets exciting contests and battles were fought, but wounds healed immediately when the fight was over.

The Chinese Paradise glittered and sparkled on a mountain high above the clouds. Gods lived in mansions of gold by a Lake of Gems near an orchard of peach trees. These peaches gave one immortality—life unending. (Mortals die, immortals don't.)

From the Heavens, down from the skies, came terrible blows; fire, flood, blizzard and thunderbolt. Why? "Look up! Can't you see the flash of a flaming sword? The gods are fighting. Listen! Hear the roars of awful anger! The gods are mad . . . perhaps at us."

Hell is always underground. Hell is always horrible.

A cobra guarded the Egyptian Hall of the Dead at the bottom of long, gloomy tunnels. Once inside, a man's heart was weighed and if it did not balance against the weight of the feather of truth, a Crocodile Fiend devoured the wicked Egyptian. The Land of Shades, according to the Inca Indians, was in the center of the earth reigned over by Supay the Shadow, god of death.

The Norse dead needed heavy shoes for the terrifying journey down through icy streams and a cave of snakes. At the crystal bridge a skeleton collected a toll of blood. At Hel-gate, the entrance to the lower regions, a fierce dog demanded Hel-cake. Deeper down a gnawing serpent waited in a great roiling cauldron surrounded by piles of cast-out bones.

The Greek Hades was even worse. Around it ran a river of fire, a river of tears and the black River Styx. Grumpy Charon, who ferried the dead across in a leaking old boat, collected coins from the pale sad passengers. Guarding the entrance was fearsome Cerberus, the three-headed watchdog. Inside, the blindfolded Goddess of Justice weighed incoming souls in her scales. The good went off to the Elysian Fields and the bad went down to punishment. Screams and wails and moans of the tortured echoed from the pits where sinners filled and refilled bottomless water vessels and were tied to a wheel revolved over flames. There Tantalus suffered, up to his neck in water, unable to drink. There another sinner rolled a huge boulder uphill, over and over and over again.

Other dark Underworlds and hot Infernos were imagined and dreaded; good places to stay out of.

CHARON

CERBERUS

JUSTICE

HEL-GATE

HEL
GODDESS OF UNDERWORLD

OAK AND MISTLETOE

DRUIDS

MAYPOLE

STONEHENGE – ENGLAND

BLACK MAGIC

ABOUT IDOLS AND SUPERSTITIONS Primitive man thought that animals and trees had feelings, just as he did. He begged the rabbit's pardon before he killed it for dinner and apologized to the tree when he chopped his firewood. Very important to him were fruit and meat, rice and corn, and the coming of spring. All these important things were admired and honored and appeared as offerings on his altar; a dressed-up ear of corn, a carved wooden calf, a pomegranate. In all countries, at one time or another, a particular tree was believed sacred; in Egypt, the fig; in India, the date palm; in China, the peach; in Japan, the willow; in Europe, the oak. Dancing around a Maypole continues a custom of ages ago—a joyful service beneath a tree that unfolded its leaves and came to life again. Voodoo superstition, also ages old, is not joyous. It tries, with spells and charms and potions, with candles, curses and dark fear, to direct the fate of men.

ABOUT ALTARS AND TEMPLES The altar at first was a low mud table; the temple, a circle of stones or trees. As hunter became farmer, then farmer became builder, the altar rose higher; on a neat pile of blocks, on a platform with steps, open to the skies. It was encircled by pillars, then covered by a roof, and lastly, enclosed by walls—the earliest church.

ABOUT MEETINGS AND WORSHIPING Living in groups now, people all went together to celebrate the first day of spring, the planting of seeds and the fall harvest. In times of trouble, a terrible drought for instance, they gathered together to beg for rain and to pray.

ABOUT SACRIFICE They tried to figure out what would please Whoever decided their fate. They said, "Let us DO something, GIVE something; show our good intentions. Let us burn this sandalwood; the sweet smell will rise to heaven. Let us raise our voices in cries, chants, songs; the Power Above may hear us. Let us kill this white chicken, this snowy lamb—a fine present. Let us offer something dear to us; a finger, a heart, a child, life itself. Give! Sacrifice! Give food, flowers, incense, prayers, and service and good deeds."

They were primitive, sometimes cruel, but kind to their children (they never spanked them). And they were religious—in their way. They looked to the sky, toward the Great Spirit, Manitou. They gathered together, clean from the steam bath, and gave what they could; baskets of corn and pretty prayer sticks trimmed with colored feathers. They held up the red clay pipe of peace. They asked for help and tried to do right.

Of course at that time there were no barometers, no weather balloons. The Indian knew nothing about warm air masses and cold fronts; he imagined a huge black Thunderbird darkened the sky. He had no X-Ray machine. When someone was desperately sick, he called his doctor, the Medicine Man, who tried with screams and charms and a horrible mask to drive away the bad thing that was causing the pain. The special herbs he brought (we still use some of them in our pills) probably did more good than the fussing, but he brought comfort and help to the anxious family. He would cure if he could; he was doctor, friend, priest and psychoanalyst, all in one.

THE CREATION OF THE WORLD according to the Indians. The White Old Man, meaning elderly, not white-skinned, father of the sun, the moon, the stars and the winds; father of the Thunderbird and animal brothers, looked down through a hole in the sky upon the earth and the waters. He bid the wind enter an ear of yellow corn. It breathed, moved, became a man. He bid the wind enter an ear of white corn. It breathed, moved, became a woman.

INDIAN LEGEND There were many repeated tales in which wonderful, unexplainable things—miracles—happened. One tells of help from the skies. Hiawatha, the great Chieftain, on a peaceful journey found his way blocked by a large lake. While he stood there wishing he had brought along his canoe, the sky grew dark with the whirring wings of thousands of ducks. Down they dipped and dived and drank. In no time at all the water was gone and Hiawatha crossed the dry lake bowl that shone and sparkled with pearls and bits of shell.

AN INDIAN PRAYER Ho. Ye sun, moon, stars, all ye that move in the heavens. Ho. Ye winds, clouds, rain, mist, all ye that move in the air. Consent ye, I implore . . .

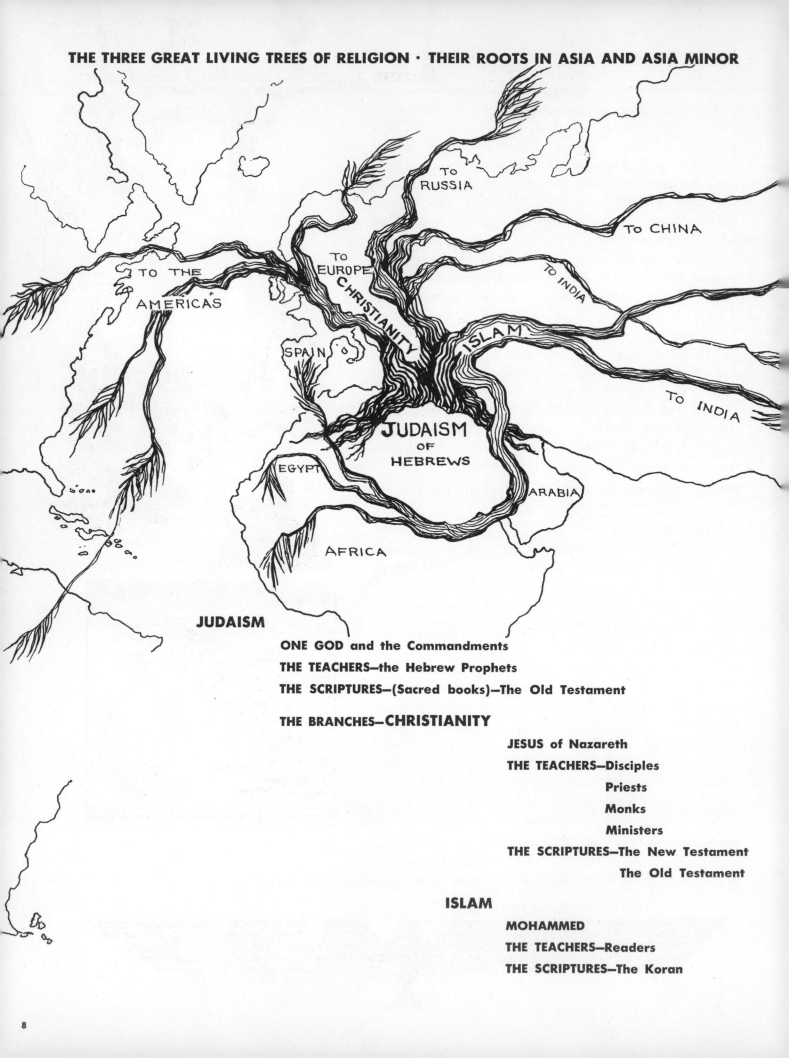

THE THREE GREAT LIVING TREES OF RELIGION · THEIR ROOTS IN ASIA AND ASIA MINOR

TO RUSSIA

TO CHINA

TO EUROPE

TO INDIA

TO THE AMERICAS

CHRISTIANITY

ISLAM

SPAIN

TO INDIA

JUDAISM OF HEBREWS

EGYPT

ARABIA

AFRICA

JUDAISM

ONE GOD and the Commandments

THE TEACHERS—the Hebrew Prophets

THE SCRIPTURES—(Sacred books)—The Old Testament

THE BRANCHES—CHRISTIANITY

JESUS of Nazareth

THE TEACHERS—Disciples

Priests

Monks

Ministers

THE SCRIPTURES—The New Testament

The Old Testament

ISLAM

MOHAMMED

THE TEACHERS—Readers

THE SCRIPTURES—The Koran

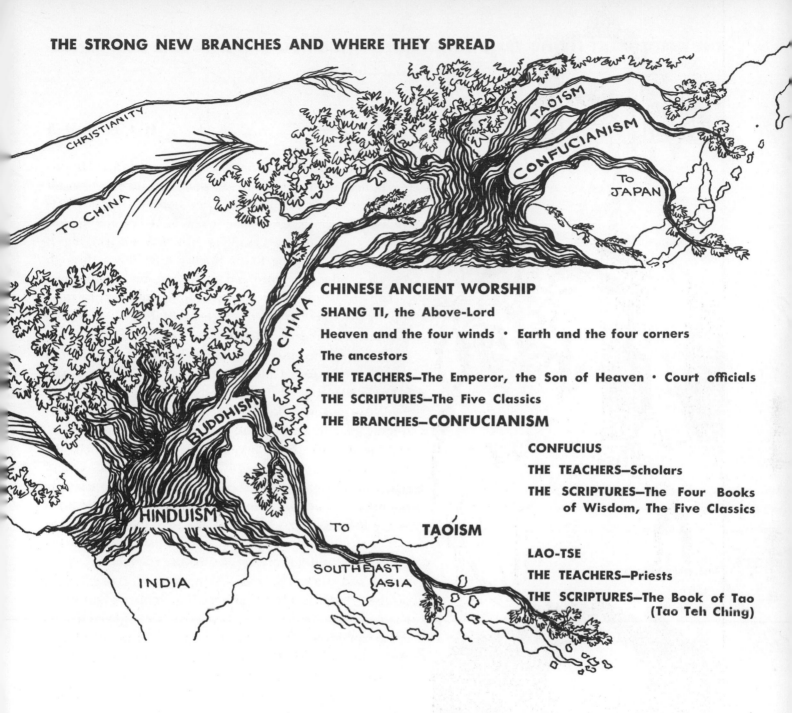

CHINESE ANCIENT WORSHIP

SHANG TI, the Above-Lord

Heaven and the four winds · Earth and the four corners

The ancestors

THE TEACHERS—The Emperor, the Son of Heaven · Court officials

THE SCRIPTURES—The Five Classics

THE BRANCHES—CONFUCIANISM

> **CONFUCIUS**
>
> **THE TEACHERS—Scholars**
>
> **THE SCRIPTURES—The Four Books of Wisdom, The Five Classics**
>
> **LAO-TSE**
>
> **THE TEACHERS—Priests**
>
> **THE SCRIPTURES—The Book of Tao (Tao Teh Ching)**

HINDUISM

> **BRAHMĀ, Supreme Being**
>
> **THE TEACHERS——Brāhman priests**
>
> **THE SCRIPTURES—Vedas, Brāhmanas, Upanishads, the Epics**
>
> **THE BRANCHES—BUDDHISM**
>
> > **BUDDHA**
> >
> > **THE TEACHERS—Monks**
> >
> > **THE SCRIPTURES—Triptaka (Three books)**

Bells ring and drums throb, every day in India. Hindus everywhere, in the temple, at home and on the road all bow their heads in worship. They believe God is everywhere in everything; in the river, in trees and plants, in birds and in animals. Very old and unchanging is their religion, flowing like a mighty river down through the ages collecting more and more customs and ideas.

The roads are never empty of pilgrims making their way to the sacred river, the Ganges. Holy men along the way are honored and fed by the passers-by. Cows and monkeys too, because of the parts they played in the old legends, are regarded affectionately and cannot be harmed.

On special days of the year festivals and processions are held. All join in following a religious figure borne aloft; singing, playing flutes, beating drums and carrying torches. On the day for remembering those who have died, the Hindus decorate their doorways with colored flowers and lights to welcome them; then set afloat on the river tiny lighted rafts, bidding them farewell. Celebrating the birth of the baby Krishna or Vishnu, the preserver of life, they gather at midnight before the doors of the temple bearing gifts of rice and flowers to place before the cradle.

Old and unchanging, too, is their way of life. Sitting on the ground is a habit in very hot countries; sitting in chairs is more comfortable where floors are cold and drafty. A turban protects one's head from the sun's torrid rays and loose white clothes are sensible in a sun-beaten land. A cool dim temple is a place of refuge and stories carved into stone last for ages in a climate where wood and paper rot and dry to dust.

HINDU HALO

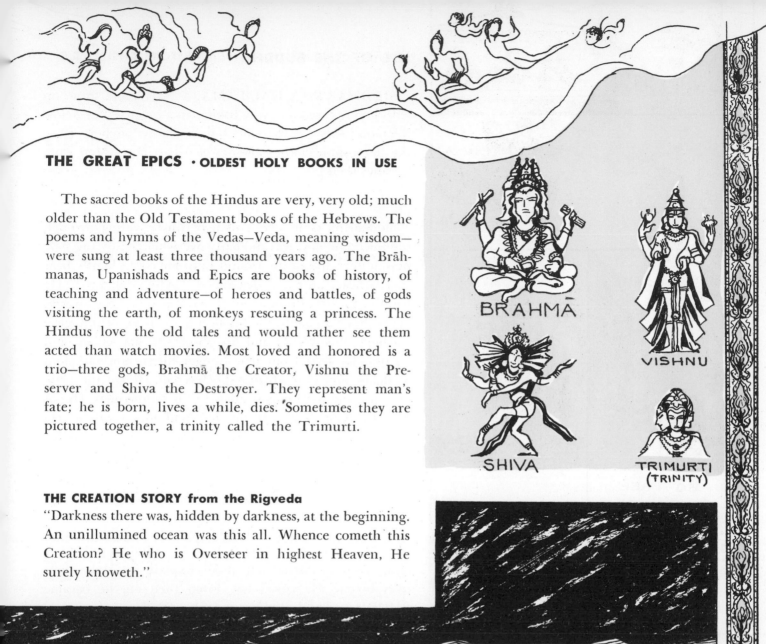

THE GREAT EPICS · OLDEST HOLY BOOKS IN USE

The sacred books of the Hindus are very, very old; much older than the Old Testament books of the Hebrews. The poems and hymns of the Vedas—Veda, meaning wisdom—were sung at least three thousand years ago. The Brāhmanas, Upanishads and Epics are books of history, of teaching and adventure—of heroes and battles, of gods visiting the earth, of monkeys rescuing a princess. The Hindus love the old tales and would rather see them acted than watch movies. Most loved and honored is a trio—three gods, Brahmā the Creator, Vishnu the Preserver and Shiva the Destroyer. They represent man's fate; he is born, lives a while, dies. Sometimes they are pictured together, a trinity called the Trimurti.

BRAHMĀ

VISHNU

SHIVA

TRIMURTI
(TRINITY)

THE CREATION STORY from the Rigveda

"Darkness there was, hidden by darkness, at the beginning. An unillumined ocean was this all. Whence cometh this Creation? He who is Overseer in highest Heaven, He surely knoweth."

A HINDU PRAYER

Great Soul, Thou art woman, Thou art man, and the dark blue bee. Thou art the thundercloud, the seasons and the sea. Thou from whom all worlds are born.

Hinduism is a religion and a way of living. Hinduism is peaceful, accepting things—good or bad—as they are, hoping for a kinder fate in another life. No one bothered much about the misery of the sick and poor until Siddhartha Gautama was born and became the great leader and teacher called Buddha.

BO TREE

LIFE OF THE BUDDHA · 560 BEFORE CHRIST, B.C.

SIDDHARTHA GAUTAMA, a Raja's son, grew up with loving care and every luxury in a green valley below the mountains. He rode fine horses, learned archery, wore the finest-spun clothes and jeweled earrings. (Men wore earrings then.)

Siddhartha Gautama, a man of thirty, riding through the town one day, was suddenly overwhelmed by the sickness, misery and death around him. He could hardly bear it. His heart hurt and demanded, "Why *is* all this?" He had to get away, think about it and try to find the answer. He whispered goodbye to his sleeping wife and child, gave his horse, his clothes and his jewelry to his servant and set out. He found out how hunger hurts, how sackcloth scratches, how stones bruise shoeless feet. He saw the kindness and the harshness of man to his fellow man. He sat and he thought and he puzzled, and forgot to eat. He pondered the meaning of life and death, the reasons for good and bad; the gift of happiness and the burden of sorrow.

One day, a sudden clear light shed upon the dark problems he had been turning over in his mind; now all was clear. Now could he help men? Explain it? Make their lives better? He could try. From then on, he became BUDDHA, The Enlightened One.

Buddha, the Teacher, walked the dusty roads of India, urging a new way of life; promising freedom from trouble and care. Disregard greedy desires and be content within; put an end to hate and malice and be at peace with yourself; this life is but a fleeting moment in a great ever-revolving universe, he counseled. His smiling serenity, simplicity and wisdom made him beloved by his followers, by the crowds in the villages and by the rulers. When he lay dying he told his sorrowful monks that they needed no teacher, no guiding light, if they would "hold fast to the truth as a lamp."

LET YOUR HEARTS BE FILLED WITH BOUNDLESS LOVE FOR ALL CREATURES GREAT AND SMALL.——BUDDHA

BUDDHISM

Monks with shaven heads, dressed in yellow robes, carried on his work in monasteries. His teachings were copied and reading and writing were taught. The great Emperor Ashoka of India became a Buddhist and built hospitals, public gardens and fountains. He sent monks out to educate, not only his people, but the people of Tibet, Siam, China, Burma, Manchuria and Turkestan. Buddhism spread down to Ceylon, out to Korea and over to Japan.

A name and a memory might not last, so Buddha's likeness was carved in enduring stone. His face always wears a calm smile, his hand is open and giving and on his head is a headdress of snails. It was said that while he meditated motionless in the hot sun, the small creatures crawled up and protected him. Stories in pictures were hammered and chiseled on walls and rocks all over India. When people love and admire, they want to express their feelings; do something or give something. Trimmings of white flowers, incense, prayer papers and prayer wheels were added to ceremonies honoring Buddha. Shelters, umbrellas and temples were built above the image of the man who taught that religion is within—in one's heart and soul.

For many centuries Buddhism was strong in India, then lost to other ideas, old and new. But it still survives in most of Asia.

BIRTH OF THE BUDDHA

Told and retold were legends of Buddha's birth. In a dream, the lovely Maja was carried by four angels to a far-off place where she heard an unseen chorus sing, "Rejoice, O Queen, a mighty son has been born to you." The King summoned sixty-four wise Brahmin priests to a magnificent feast and asked them to interpret his wife's dream. There followed the silence of sixty-four thinking, then the murmuring of sixty-four conferring, and finally the announcement—"You will have a son who will become the Monarch of the Universe."

The Queen's every wish and whim were granted and when she expressed a desire to visit her old home, a thousand courtiers rode beside the golden palanquin while four guardian angels flew above. When the long procession stopped for rest and water, Maja wandered off to a shady grove. There, surrounded by sweet-smelling blossoms and rustling leaves, amidst the singing and warbling of many birds, the baby Buddha was born.

SYMBOLS

Spring—PEONY

Summer—LOTUS

Fall—CRYSANTHEMUM

Winter—PLUM

LONG LIFE	IMMORTALITY	RICHES	PEACE	100 CHILDREN

CHINESE · CEREMONIOUS · Cultured and Classic

Chinese customs and ceremonies date from ancient times. When most of the world was young and savage, China was writing and painting and weaving beautiful silks. Worship and manners have followed the very old sacred books, the Classics. Incense sticks and candles, flowers and tablets in memory of parents and grandparents are kept on altars in every home. Artists with the brush, their writing began as pictures. Color and design were important to them and they gave meaning to both; blue represents heaven, yellow, the earth, red, the life-giving sun—warm red for the temple roof, gay red for firecrackers, happy red eggs to announce the birth of a baby; red curtains for the bride's carriage and red papers for their prayers.

The Chinese write their prayers. When they kneel to pray they bow their heads—all the way to the floor. Almost everything is done with a this-is-an-occasion air, just as it has been done for centuries; greeting spring in happy processions, bowing toward the four corners, North, East, West and South, whence come warm winds and gentle rains; wishing good luck with sweet grass, flowers and prosperity cakes, chasing bad luck with firecrackers; giving thanks to the kitchen god, for the fire that warms the house and cooks the food. Bowing, thanking and good manners make daily life pleasant and peaceful.

A CHINESE PRAYER from the Book of Odes

How great is God, the ruler of men below! God created the myriad people. All men are good at birth but not many remain so to the end.

THE SON OF HEAVEN

When the Flowery Kingdom had an Emperor, he led the religious rites and was spokesman for his people to the Power Above. Bronze dragons guard the temples of China from evil, and a five-toed dragon (the others had four) was the official insignia of the Imperial Palace. Two dogs that look like lions guard the doorways of homes.

GUARDIAN DRAGON

GUARDIAN OF HOMES
DOGS OF FU

THE CHINESE CREATION STORY

There was nothing, then something—a tumult and roar as if from a great giant dying. From his last long groan rumbled the thunder; from his last heaving breath rushed the wind. Out from his right eye shot the hot, bright sun; from his left eye, closing, the moon. From his veins flowed great rivers and from his hair sprang the thick forests.

HEAVEN AND EARTH and YANG AND YIN

Off beyond the clouds, in the blue firmament of Heaven, is the Above-Lord, Shang Ti, Supreme Ruler, creator and controller of all.

Below-the-sky, Chinese word for earth, is a world keeping a balance of half and half, called Yang and Yin. Half the earth is light—Yang, while half the earth is dark—Yin.

There is man and woman, life and death, spirit and body. Good balances evil; joy—sorrow; fire—water; strength—weakness. A true balance is hard to keep. There must be rain or the plants will wither; there must be sun or the garden won't grow. If one were not cold and numb, would the warmth of the fire feel so good? Man must hope and strive for not too much and not too little—moderation.

YIN AND YANG

HELP AND CONSOLE
YOUR NEIGHBORS
AND RELATIVES
IN NEED

RESPECT
FOR THE ELDERS
AND RITES IN THE
FAMILY MUST BE
MAINTAINED

Confucius, the little gentle gentleman, visited around, talking and writing and teaching. His students listened, the rulers listened and the people listened.

He offered calm good sense and advice. He explained the Five Classics, China's books of history, law, custom and religion which at that time were more than a thousand years old.

"We learn these Classics, we observe them, we go through the proper motions; we bow, light incense, write prayers. But do we live them? How do we act in the streets, in the shop, in our homes?" he said. "Man is born good, but ignorance makes him bad; he knows no better. Let us have patience, let us teach him and make him better. Then we will have a better world."

THE BOOKS OF
SONGS   CHANGES
HISTORY   SEASONS
CEREMONIES

Confucius' four Books of Wisdom are honored in China; an educated person knows every word. Confucianism, living as Confucius advocated, respecting the teachings, is called a religion.

LEARNING

DURING A DISPUTE
THE GENTLEMAN
TALKS, BUT THE
SCOUNDREL ACTS
WITH HANDS

TEACH YOUR CHILDREN
WITH GOOD BOOKS—
NO MATTER
HOW STUPID
THEY MAY BE

WHAT YOU DO NOT WANT DONE TO YOURSELF, DO NOT DO TO OTHERS.—CONFUCIUS

CHIEF	SOULS	TRAVELERS	HOMES	MUSICIANS	ACTORS
FAN	BAMBOO RODS	GOURD	LOTUS	FLUTE	CASTANETS

SICK

SWORD

FLORISTS

BASKET

According to folklore these eight Chinese guardians, or patron saints, who affectionately watch over the small doings of daily life, live on a floating island in the Eastern Sea of the sky—Peachtree Island, to be exact. The peach is a symbol of immortality, life unending, undying. Pictures and symbols are dear to the Chinese. Flowers represent the seasons: the peony, Spring; the lotus, Summer; the chrysanthemum, Fall; the plum, Winter. Decorated bowls and screens carry messages; good health. peace, many children.

A floating ribbon is a sign of something precious, holy and sacred.

BUDDHISM INTO CHINA

By sea, and across the mountains through Tibet Buddhist monks brought the story and teachings of Buddha. The books were translated by scholars, studied carefully, and considered good by the Emperor. Buddhism was welcomed and added to the earlier religions and on the roads appeared shrines and pagodas, images of the serene Buddha and the Queen of Heaven, Holy Mother of Mercy, Kwanyin.

PAGODA

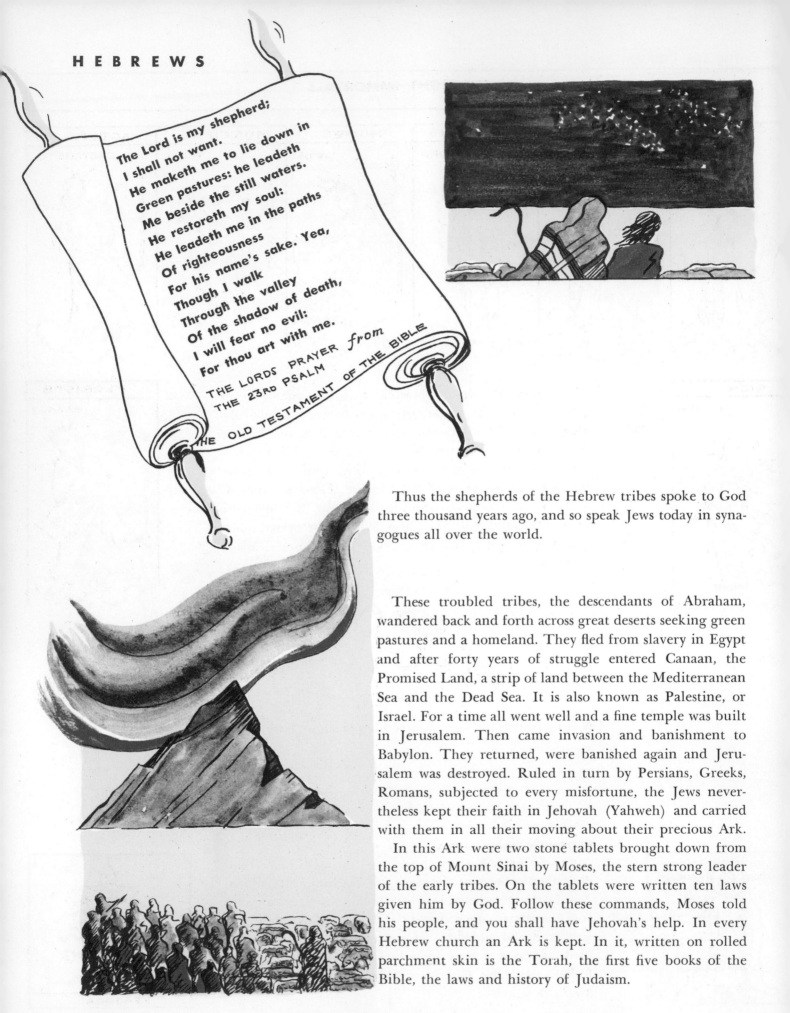

HEBREWS

The Lord is my shepherd;
I shall not want.
He maketh me to lie down in
Green pastures: he leadeth
Me beside the still waters.
He restoreth my soul:
He leadeth me in the paths
Of righteousness
For his name's sake. Yea,
Though I walk
Through the valley
Of the shadow of death,
I will fear no evil:
For thou art with me.

THE LORDS PRAYER *from*
THE 23RD PSALM
THE OLD TESTAMENT OF THE BIBLE

Thus the shepherds of the Hebrew tribes spoke to God three thousand years ago, and so speak Jews today in synagogues all over the world.

These troubled tribes, the descendants of Abraham, wandered back and forth across great deserts seeking green pastures and a homeland. They fled from slavery in Egypt and after forty years of struggle entered Canaan, the Promised Land, a strip of land between the Mediterranean Sea and the Dead Sea. It is also known as Palestine, or Israel. For a time all went well and a fine temple was built in Jerusalem. Then came invasion and banishment to Babylon. They returned, were banished again and Jerusalem was destroyed. Ruled in turn by Persians, Greeks, Romans, subjected to every misfortune, the Jews nevertheless kept their faith in Jehovah (Yahweh) and carried with them in all their moving about their precious Ark.

In this Ark were two stone tablets brought down from the top of Mount Sinai by Moses, the stern strong leader of the early tribes. On the tablets were written ten laws given him by God. Follow these commands, Moses told his people, and you shall have Jehovah's help. In every Hebrew church an Ark is kept. In it, written on rolled parchment skin is the Torah, the first five books of the Bible, the laws and history of Judaism.

THE TEN COMMANDMENTS

1. Thou shalt have no other gods.
2. Thou shalt not make any graven image.
3. Thou shalt not name the Lord in vain.
4. The Sabbath, keep it holy.
5. Honor thy father and mother.
6. Thou shalt not kill.
7. Thou shalt not commit faithlessness.
8. Thou shalt not steal.
9. Thou shalt not lie against thy neighbor.
10. Thou shalt not covet thy neighbor's things.

THE CREATION OF THE WORLD

In the beginning God created the heaven and earth. And the earth was without form and darkness was upon the face of the waters.

And God said:

Let there be light; and there was light. And God called the light Day, and the darkness he called Night.

Let there be a firmament; and it was so. And God called the firmament Heaven.

Let there be lights in the firmament of heaven. And God made two great lights; the greater light to rule the day, and the lesser light to rule the night.

Let the dry land appear; and it was so. And God called the dry land Earth; and the waters the Seas.

Let the earth bring forth grass, the herb and the fruit tree.

Let there be the moving creature that hath life. And God created great whales and winged fowl. And God made the beast of the earth and cattle and every thing that creepeth.

Let us make man; and let him have domination over the fish of the sea, and over the fowl of the air and over the cattle, and over all the earth, and over every creeping thing. So God created man in his own image; male and female, created he them.

And God saw everything that he had made, and behold it was very good. Thus the heavens and earth were finished. And he rested on the seventh day from all his work which he had made.—Genesis, Old Testament

This is the beginning as told by Hebrew father to son down through the centuries. This is the beginning as written on clay and scraps of skin. This is the beginning page of the Old Testament of the Bible, which is also the first 1000 pages of the Holy Bible of Christians. This Book of Books, translated into almost every language, became the foundation of the beliefs and faith and worship of half the world. In it are the prayers and psalms once wailed in camps and temples; now sung in churches, homes, and schools.

JUDAISM

However, far from the **TEMPLE** in Jerusalem, groups of Hebrews observed their Sabbath Saturday. They gathered together to worship, to chant the Psalms and listen to the Books. The meeting places, damp cellars in Europe, peaked Chinese houses, vine-covered arbors of Africa, were called **SYNAGOGUES**.

Though the families spoke the language used about them, the children also learned to read and write Hebrew. Thus, from generation to generation the Rabbis, the teachers, preserved the link to other scattered Jews throughout the world. The belief in one God was never lost; despite wars, migrations, isolation and persecution.

To this day, as of old, portions of the Pentateuch are read at weekly services; the whole Scripture is reviewed in a year. Boys are named when eight days old, usually in honor of a relative no longer living. At thirteen, having studied the Books and the Law, they are received as adults with ceremony, the Bar-Mizvah. They are given the symbols of shawl and Tefilin, and the responsibility of carrying on the Faith. Heads remain covered during Hebrew services in humble respect to the presence of the Lord. Circumcision and dietary rules date from customs established long ago.

The blowing of the ram's horn at Sunset on Rosh Hashanah announces the New Year. Ten solemn days follow, during which the Jew considers his joys and troubles, his sins and his goodness; makes penitence and resolutions, and fasts on Yom Kippur, the Day of Atonement.

In the spring, Passover recalls the flight from Egypt. The story is read, thanks are given, symbols of the hurried packing and moving are on the table; bone of the lamb, parsley, the herbs, and matzoth, the unrisen bread. Chanukah, a Festival of Lights in wintertime, celebrates, with the lighting of many candles and delicious things to eat, another escape from tyranny and oppression to religious freedom.

IN THE BIBLE are wonder tales—exciting adventures, battles, murder, miracles and strange happenings.

ADAM AND EVE The first man and woman created by the Lord should have been content in the wonderful Garden of Eden; they had everything one could possibly desire. Only one thing was forbidden, the fruit of the Tree of Knowledge. Evil lurked there too, even in that perfect place; the sly serpent tempted Eve and urged her to eat the forbidden fruit. She persuaded Adam, and all three hid guiltily from God's anger. Because they could not resist doing what they knew was wrong, they were cast out into a world of work and hardship.

MOSES The unwavering faith of Moses overcame discouragement and defeat as he led the Hebrew tribes out from Egypt. With the Lord's help, when they suffered hunger and thirst, he produced water from rock and manna from the fields. He prodded the straggling nomads on and on, and by a miracle, got them safely across the Red Sea a few lengths ahead of pursuing soldiers. He inspired them when he climbed through smoke and lightning and thunderings to the mountaintop and returned to the trembling tribes with word from God.

NOAH When God decided to destroy the squabbling, sinful people of the world and start over again, he forewarned Noah, a good man, of the great flood to come. Noah built an ark for his wife and his sons, and their wives, and he took on board two of every living thing when "the windows of heaven were opened. And rain was upon the earth for forty days and forty nights." They were ready, when the water subsided, to go forth and fill the silent empty earth with the shouts of children, the bleating of lambs and the whirr of wings.

SAMSON Born with extraordinary God-given strength in order to deliver the children of Israel from the Philistines, Samson was betrayed by a woman he loved, Delilah. She told his secret—his strength lay in his hair—to the enemy and they cut his hair and imprisoned him. When thousands gathered to mock the captive giant, Samson came forth, his hair grown again, and called upon the Lord to strengthen him. He grasped the middle pillars on which the building stood and the walls and the roof of great stone blocks crashed down, killing all—Samson, too.

DANIEL While captive in Babylon, Daniel was called to the court of Nebuchadnezzar to interpret a dream which had the wise men baffled. The King was pleased with Daniel's prophecy and made him a great man at the palace; but the princes were not pleased and plotted his downfall with an edict forbidding kneeling except to the King. Daniel, steadfast to his God, knelt and prayed toward Jerusalem as usual. He was seized, thrown into the lions' den, but emerged unharmed. Thereupon Nebuchadnezzar proclaimed that Daniel's God, who had delivered him from the lions' den, would henceforth be the one and only God worshiped in all the Kingdom.

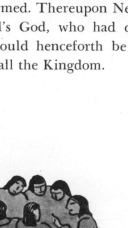

JOSEPH The youngest son of Jacob was hated by his brothers because of his boastful dreams of superiority and because his father favored him most. His eleven brothers plotted his death, but relented, and sold him to merchants Egypt-bound. They brought back Joseph's coat of many colors stained with the blood of a sheep, and his father mourned, believing him killed. In Egypt, "the Lord was with Joseph," and he became a favorite of the Pharaoh. In time, his brothers arrived in Egypt but did not recognize him. Joseph forgave them and helped them and they brought their aging sorrowful father to a joyous reunion with his long-lost son.

ELIJAH Elijah, the Prophet, waged unceasing war throughout all his days against wickedness and the worship of Baal. Alone on a hill he withstood the demands of the soldiers of the King and was helped by the fire of the Lord. "And it came to pass, when the Lord would take . . . Elijah into heaven, that Elijah went with Elisha from Gilgal . . . and they two stood by Jordan. And Elijah took his mantle . . . and smote the waters, and they were divided hither and thither, so that they two went over on dry ground. . . . And it came to pass, as they still went on, and talked, that behold, there appeared a chariot of fire, and horses of fire, and parted them both asunder, and Elijah went up by a whirlwind into heaven."

RUTH Ruth, a kind and gentle widow, left her homeland, the Moab country, and helped her husband's aged, lonesome mother return to her people in Bethlehem. Her words of loyalty are often repeated—"Whither thou goest, I will go . . . thy people shall be my people." On the long journey she trailed the harvesters, picking up grain to feed her frail mother-in-law. The Hebrew townspeople welcomed the foreigner into their midst. Her devotion and sweetness were noticed by Boaz, a wealthy landowner, who asked Ruth to be his wife.

DAVID David, a young shepherd noted for his songs and sweet music, was sent for to comfort the ailing King Saul. When Goliath, the huge armored giant of the Philistines' army, challenged the Israelites to send forth their mightiest warrior, David volunteered. He was slim and young but had killed both lion and bear in his sheepherding days. He refused shield and sword and went forth with only five stones and a slingshot, declaring that the Lord who had delivered him from the lion's paw would help him. One stone shot straight and true into the giant's forehead, killing him. David led the armies on to other victories and married a daughter of the aging King. When he became King of Judah, the Elders of Israel asked him to be their king too—thus uniting the Hebrew Kingdoms.

KING SOLOMON The Kingdom of Israel, united by David, became splendid and powerful during the reign of his son, Solomon. The magnificent temple to Jehovah was built and the people rejoiced in the wise judgment of their ruler. Many of the proverbs are his words of wisdom and the Songs of Solomon have great beauty—"For lo, the winter is past, the rain is over and gone; the flowers appear on the earth; the time of the singing of birds is come, and the voice of the turtle [turtledove] is heard in our land." . . .

JOB The sufferings and misfortunes of Job, who was a good man, were hard to bear and hard to understand. His oxen were stolen, his stables and sheep burned, his servants and camels slain, and his children were killed when his house caved in. He grieved and he mourned and he sought an answer; but he blamed himself, not the Lord. What Job thought and said; what his friends, trying to comfort him, advised; and the answers of the Lord out of the Whirlwind is called "The Great Debate." Job's patience and humility and faith were, in the end, rewarded with a new home, new stables and animals and ten new children.

JONÁH Jonah was directed by the Lord to go and change the wicked selfish ways of the city of Nineveh, but he fled in the opposite direction. His ship was overtaken by a great wind, and Jonah, to appease the Lord and calm the seas, was cast overboard and was immediately swallowed by a great whale. He repented his cowardly flight and he prayed and he prayed for three nights and days. "And the Lord spake unto the fish, and it vomited out Jonah upon the dry land." Jonah hastened to Nineveh and warned the people of the Lord's threat to destroy them. They turned from their evil way, they fasted and dressed in sackcloth; they believed God, and the city was spared.

THE GREAT PROPHETS AND THE BOOK

The prophets and The Book held the tribes together, kept alive the faith; foretelling a future greatness and promising God's aid.

In times of trouble the Prophets encouraged the people, predicting victory and a Land of Plenty.

MOSES led them from slavery in Egypt, repeating God's message: that God would smite Egypt with plagues, would destroy Egypt, would go before his Chosen People and lead them into a good land flowing with milk and honey. They hastily packed cold lamb and flat bread dough— there was not time for it to rise—and pulled green herbs from their gardens. All these are part of the Passover Feast every spring when Jews give thanks and remember the great Exodus (the road out). After years of wandering and camping in the wilderness they finally came to the Promised Land and established a Kingdom which lasted for about five hundred years.

THE PROPHETS and THE KINGDOM and THE BOOK

In times of lazy laxness the Prophets threatened punishment.

ELIJAH warned against false gods and the heartless Queen Jezebel. He pleaded with the Hebrews to mend their ways. "How long halt ye between two opinions? if the Lord be God, follow him . . ."

AMOS thundered against soft, selfish living, the neglect of God, and of the poor. Repent, he scolded, or doom and destruction. "the Lord . . . saith thus; Wailing shall be in all streets . . . I will not hear . . . But let judgment run down as waters . . ."

ISAIAH called for strength, and faith in Jehovah, while war swirled round the Kingdom. He promised a bright future for Israel and the world. "Behold, a King shall reign in righteousness . . . eyes shall not be dim . . . ears shall hearken. The heart shall understand . . . the tongue speak plainly. The people that walked in darkness have seen a great light . . . For unto us a child is born, unto us a son is given: and the government shall be upon his shoulder; and his name shall be called Wonderful, Counselor, The mighty God, The everlasting Father, The Prince of Peace."

PROPHETS

MAJOR	MINOR
Isaiah	Hosea
Jeremiah	Joel
Ezekiel	Amos
	Obadiah
	Jonah
	Micah
	Nahum
	Habakkuk
	Zephaniah
	Haggai
	Zechariah
	Malachi

JEREMIAH urged the heedless, "Amend your ways and your doings." He prophesied banishment. "And this whole land shall be a desolation . . . and these nations shall serve the king of Babylon seventy years."

Armies descended on the Kingdom of Judah, Jerusalem was captured, Hebrews were carted off to Babylon. Jerusalem was destroyed.

THE PROPHETS' PROPHECIES HAD COME TRUE.

In times of despair, the Prophets offered hope.

EZEKIEL comforted them as best he could, recalled their past and foretold a brighter future when the Lord "will bring them to their own land, will set up one shepherd over them." In Babylon they learned to write and in sorrow and yearning they began to collect and record on bits of clay and scraps of parchment the words of their Prophets, the long history of the travels and troubles of the scattered tribes.

ISAIAH II promised the discouraged exiles a return to Jerusalem and a gentle God who would "feed his flock . . . will hold thine hand and will keep thee." And they did return under Persian rule and set about building a new Temple. Greek armies marched in, then Romans conquered the Greeks and Herod, half Jewish, was appointed ruler.

The Hebrews recalled and repeated the Words of the Prophets in their meeting places. Children listened to Isaiah's prophecy of long ago.

"For unto us a child is born, unto us a son is given . . . his name shall be called . . . The Prince of Peace."

Was this he? This little Jewish boy born in Bethlehem, growing up in the small town of Nazareth, hammering nails in Joseph's carpentry shop? Was this he—the twelve-year-old, visiting the temple in Jerusalem at Passover, discussing with priests and grown men the Hebrew laws and prophecies?

Was this he? This young man listening to John the Baptist's wild warnings of the end of the world; washing away sins, being baptized in the river Jordan?

Was this he? wondered the villagers and fishermen of Galilee, when he came among them praising God, the forgiving Father of *all* mankind. Was this he? asked the crowds in Jerusalem when he and his followers knocked over the counters of the noisy money changers in the temple court.

Was he God's messenger, the hope of the world? Yes, thought the poor and humble. Was he a dangerous trouble-maker, another rabble rouser like John the Baptist who had lost his head? Yes, said the Hebrew Elders and priests, the Romans might close the Temple, even destroy it.

Was he doomed? Yes, he must die.

Was he just another lawbreaker as he hung beside two thieves? Yes, said the Roman soldiers and most Jews.

Was he the Saviour sent by the Lord? Yes, said a few. He is dying for all of us. He is paying with his life for all our sins and meanness. He tried to bring brotherly love and peace to this earth. He might still do it: somehow. His body died, but his spirit lives.

WHATSOEVER YE WOULD THAT MEN SHOULD DO TO YOU, DO YE EVEN SO TO THEM—JESUS

The excitement in Jerusalem died down quickly and people went about their bargaining and trading. There were some rumors, though. Jesus' tomb was empty, the rock had been rolled back; someone had seen him rise in a cloud. His disciples came forth from hiding and said they had seen and talked with him; that he had been received into Heaven and had taken his place beside God.

Surely now there was no doubt, they argued, Jesus was God's messenger, the Messiah; God's son, holy, sacred and divine—the Christos. Over all, they proclaimed, was a Trinity (a trio, three) —God, the Father, Christ, the Son, and the Holy Ghost (Holy Spirit) .

One God. One God only, thundered the Hebrew Council, is the First Commandment—"Thou shalt have no other gods . . ." Who dares to say Jesus is up there sharing God's Glory? This was outrageous sacrilege, wicked and evil. Destroy the blasphemers, cast them out from the temple, from the town! Some faithful fled to the desert; the disciples scattered and went out to teach and preach about Jesus, the Christ.

Pursuing the Jewish Christians went Saul, later called Paul. He had grown up in far-off Tarsus and had come to Jerusalem to study Hebrew law and religion. He was smart, lively and excitable. He could not stand disloyalty to Jehovah, long the one God of his people. Fired with indignation and fury he threatened slaughter against the followers of Jesus and set out to the synagogues to capture and bring them, bound, back to Jerusalem.

JESUS' DISCIPLES Peter, Andrew, James, John, Philip, Bartholomew, Thomas, Matthew, Simon, James, Thaddeus, and Judas Iscariot, who betrayed Jesus; who told the officers of the law that he was in Gethsemane.

THE RESURRECTION
'HE IS ARISEN'

XPICTOC
(CHRIST - (GREEK)

NIMBUS
(HALO)

IHS

IHS - First three letters Jesus

INRI — *Iesus Nazarenus Rex Idaeorum*
Jesus of Nazareth, King of the Jews

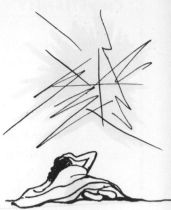

PAUL The Christian—PAUL The Apostle—SAINT PAUL

On his way to Damascus, something strange happened to Saul. There was a flash of shimmering light, and suddenly he lay in the road, stunned and blinded.

He had heard the voice of Jesus, he told the men who picked him up, and he forthwith joined the Christians instead of arresting them. Straightway he preached Christ in the synagogues; proclaimed that "He is the Son of God."

HE WENT ABOUT, SPREADING THE "GOOD NEWS,"

WAS CHASED,   **JOURNEYED TO SMALL GREEK TOWNS,**   **WAS PUT OUT, WAS HUNTED,**

RETURNED TO JERUSALEM,   **WAS IMPRISONED,**   **ESCAPED, WAS SHIPWRECKED,**

Nothing could stop him; threats, ridicule, punishment, hunger, weariness, nor old age.

MADE HIS WAY TO ROME.   **HE WROTE HIS EPISTLES,**   **HE WAS PERSECUTED,**

His courage and faith and glowing speech drew many new followers to the new religion; his letters to the small troubled Christian Churches kept them inspired and firm. His letters are the earliest written records of the Christian religion.

HE DIED WITH MARTYRS.

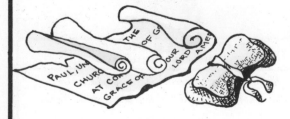

ONE HUNDRED YEARS AFTER. A.D. 100. (Anno Domini—in the year of Our Lord.)

One hundred years after Christ there were only a few scattered groups of Christians in Alexandria, along the coast of Greece, in Asia Minor and in Rome.

CHRISTIANITY · GROWING
A.D. 200—THE EARLY SAINTS

To the early Christian meetings came some Jews, some slaves, and some down-trodden Romans. They listened to the story of Jesus and were comforted; they hoped for an end of misery and awaited the Kingdom of Heaven and the second coming of the Christ. They were called saints and sometimes had little feasts together.

The Romans became alarmed. These Christians refused to honor the Emperor; they must be traitors! They talked of another Kingdom; they were plotting against the Empire! Slaves attended the meetings; there would be an uprising! The groups were growing larger; they must be stopped!

The Christians were hunted down, questioned and imprisoned. They were stoned; they were thrown to lions in the Arena while thousands cheered. Their books and letters were burned. The martyrs died by hundreds; died unafraid and smiling. This was strange. What faith could make them so brave?

The thinkers and the scholars were curious and began to read the Gospels of Matthew and John and Mark and Luke and the Epistles of Paul. They found there something solid and unifying, noble and enduring, and inspiring.

Our Father which art in heaven,
Hallowed be thy name.
Thy kingdom come.
Thy will be done in earth,
As it is in heaven.
Give us this day our daily bread:
And forgive us our debts,
As we forgive our debtors. And
Lead us not into temptation,
But deliver us from evil:
For thine is the kingdom, and
The power, and the glory, for ever.

**The Sermon on the Mount
New Testament**

A.D. 300—THE CHRISTIAN CHURCH

Seven years after Constantine the Great became Emperor of Rome, he proclaimed equality for all religions. Twelve years later the Christian Catholic church was declared official and the Nicene Creed—what they believed —formed. Seventy years later the temples and meetings of all other religions were forbidden.

Constantine, Rex

GENESIS: The beginning. Adam and his descendants.

EXODUS: Moses leads the tribes out from Egypt.

LEVITICUS: Laws and rules for conduct and worship.

NUMBERS: Names and numbers of the wandering tribes.

DEUTERONOMY: Hebrews reach the Promised Land.

JOSHUA: Battling across the Jordan. Victory. Jericho's walls came tumbling down.

JUDGES: History of leaders and triumphs and defeats. Story of Samson and Delilah. Song of Deborah.

RUTH: Romance of a loyal foreigner; poverty and riches.

SAMUEL: The first King, Saul. The Philistines. David and Goliath. Ark lost and recovered. Five hundred years of history.

KINGS: Solomon, the Temple, Queen of Sheba, Kings, Jezebel, Elijah, the Prophet.

CHRONICLES: Setbacks and successes of 500 years retold.

EZRA: Exiles return to Jerusalem.

NEHEMIAH: Rebuilding the temple.

ESTHER: Jewish girl became Persian Queen; saved her people from destruction.

JOB: His trials, misfortunes and lamentations and the debate.

PSALMS: Prayers, poems, hymns—the Psalter.
19: The Heavens declare the glory of God . . .
23: The Lord is my shepherd . . .
24: The earth is the Lord's and the fullness
    thereof . . .

PROVERBS: Short sayings of wise men.
Wisdom is better than rubies.
A soft answer turneth away wrath.
A good name is rather to be chosen than great
    riches.
Train up a child in the way he should go.

ECCLESIASTES: The Preacher: The rhythm of life. God's wisdom and judgment. "The sun also riseth and the sun goeth down . . ." "A time to be born and a time to die . . ."

SONG OF SOLOMON: Poetry of glorious true love.

ISAIAH: Prophet, warns the sinful nation; predicts destruction, captivity, restoration and the future—"Unto us a child is born . . ."

JEREMIAH: Prophet, warns of the Lord's judgment; predicts desolation.

LAMENTATIONS OF JEREMIAH: Sorrows and prayers of the Prophet. "Lord, dost thou forget us forever and forsake us . . .?"

EZEKIEL: Prophet promises the exiles return to Jerusalem.

DANIEL: A hero's courage and faith. The Lions' Den. The Fiery Furnace. The Golden Idol with feet of clay.

HOSEA: Prophet, predicts the conquest of faithless tribes.

JOEL: Prophet, warns neglectful people of the Lord's judgment. The Plague of Locusts. The Persian conquest.

AMOS: Peasant Prophet, deplores sinful luxury; predicts doom.

OBADIAH: Prophet, promises the Lord's help.

JONAH: Failure, punishment and repentance. The whale and the message to Nineveh.

MICAH: Prophet, warns of disaster; promises delivery.

NAHUM: Prophet, predicts the fall of sinful Nineveh.

HABAKKUK: Prophet, cries for the Lord's help.

ZEPHANIAH: Prophet, warns of Judgment Day.

HAGGAI: Prophet, urges rebuilding the temple

NEHEMIAH: Prophet, urges a new temple; promises the Lord's help.

MALACHI: Prophet, proclaims God's love for Israel; promises a Messenger, a Saviour, a Messiah.

THE APOCRYPHA: Books written during 400 years between Old and New Testaments, not usually included in Bibles:
Maccabees. Tobit. Judith. Susanna. Ecclesiasticus. Wisdom of Solomon. Esdras. History, and folktales and proverbs.

GOSPELS

MATTHEW: The Gospel; life and teachings of Jesus. The Nativity, Crucifixion, Resurrection. The Sermon on the Mount.

MARK: The Gospel; the life and deeds of Jesus as told to Mark by Peter. The Kingdom of Heaven on Earth.

LUKE: The Gospel; life of Jesus, the facts, dates and places, written by Luke, Gentile friend of Paul.

JOHN: The Gospel; the meaning of Christianity; God is love, the fellowship of the love of Christ; Jesus, Saviour and Light of the World.

THE ACTS: Also by Luke. Report on how the Gospel spread from Jerusalem to Greece to Rome; about Stephen, first Christian martyr.

THE EPISTLES—LETTERS FROM PAUL

ROMANS: Message to the Christians of Rome, urging courage and faith; warnings of the dangers of disputes.

CORINTHIANS: Letters from Paul to churches across the sea in Greece; advice and rules.

GALATIANS: Letter to the church in Asia Minor; hope and cheer and an outline for ideal life.

EPHESIANS: Letter from Paul, prisoner in Rome, to the church in western Asia Minor; continue strong in unity and thankful in faith.

PHILIPPIANS: Letter from Paul, still prisoner in Rome, to thank them for their message and help.

COLOSSIANS: Letter from Paul from Rome to southern Asia Minor; praise and admonitions— be humble, stay together, rich and poor.

THESSALONIANS: Letter from Paul to Greek churches; encouragement, guidance, instructions for good Christian life.

TIMOTHY: Letter to his helper, explaining rules and regulations of the church.

TITUS: Letter to his helper; advice on conducting the church.

PHILEMON: Letter from Paul asking Philemon, the Christian, to take back his runaway Christian slave.

HEBREWS: Letter from Paul from Jerusalem to Rome; affirming the power of faith and the love of Christ.

JAMES: A sermon, good, direct, simple; copied and sent all over.

PETER: Messages from the disciple of Jesus to scattered Christians; encouraging endurance of suffering and persecution.

JOHN: Three letters from John promising love and eternal life for followers of Jesus; love one another: follow good, not evil.

JUDE: Letter from Jude, servant of Jesus; warning of evil and ungodly men and the Lord's judgment.

REVELATION: THE APOCALYPSE: Vision of the Judgment Day; earthquakes, lightning and thunder; beasts and dragons; the bottomless pit and the lake of fire; trumpets and angel voices and a rainbow; the triumph of faith in Jesus and the Glory of the Kingdom of Heaven.

Adapted from the Gospels—New Testament

The angel Gabriel was sent from God unto a city of Galilee, named Nazareth, to a virgin espoused to a man whose name was Joseph; and the virgin's name was Mary. And the angel came in to her and said, Hail, the Lord is with thee: blessed art thou among women. Thou shalt bring forth a son, and shalt call his name Jesus. He shall be great, and shall be called the Son of the Highest.

And it came to pass in those days, that there went out a decree that all the world should be taxed; every one into his own city. And Joseph also went up from Galilee unto the city which is called Bethlehem with Mary his espoused wife, being great with child. And so it was, that, while they were there, she brought forth her firstborn son, and wrapped him in swaddling clothes and laid him in a manger; because there was no room for them in the inn.

And there were in the same country shepherds, keeping watch over their flocks by night. And, lo, the angel of the Lord came upon them, and the glory of the Lord shone round about them; and they were sore afraid. And the angel said unto them, Fear not; for behold, I bring you good tidings of great joy. For unto you is born this day a Saviour, which is Christ the Lord. And suddenly there was with the angel a multitude of the heavenly host praising God, and saying,
Glory to God in the highest, and on earth peace, good will toward men.—Luke

Now when Jesus was born in Bethlehem, there came wise men from the east to Jerusalem, saying, Where is he that is born King of the Jews? for we have seen his star in the east, and are come to worship him.—Matthew

Hundreds are honored by the church for their steadfast faith, good works and noble sacrifices.

SAINT PETER: The fisherman disciple of Galilee carried the word of Jesus far and near. He died in Rome with other persecuted Christians and is called the founder of the Roman Catholic Church.

SAINT GEORGE: The patron saint of England was a knight who went forth in the service of Jesus. The old tales tell of his slaying the great dragon of evil. His emblem, a red cross on a white ground, was later worn by the soldiers of the Crusades.

SAINT IGNATIUS LOYOLA: Soldier of Spain, organized an Army for Jesus, the Society of Jesus. His monasteries became centers of learning and from them monks carried Christian teaching to far-off China and the wilderness of America.

SAINT TERESA of Avila: A Spanish nun, overcame illness and opposition and founded many fine Carmelite convents. Her letters and travels, her courage and devotion, brought admiration and fame.

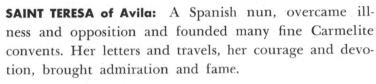

SAINT BERNARD of Menthon: Founded the monastery and hospice in a high mountain pass of the Swiss Alps. His monks and trained dogs braved blizzards to rescue lost travelers. The monastery still stands and provides refuge for wayfarers.

SAINT CHRISTOPHER: Patron saint of travelers, sought to use his great strength for a good purpose and a worthy master. After several trials, he decided that carrying pilgrims across a raging river best served the best master, Jesus.

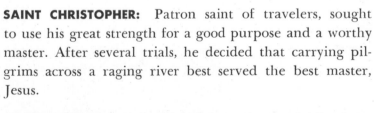

SAINT STEPHEN: Defied the Hebrew Law and joined the disciples of Jesus. He was tried by the Council and condemned; was stoned to death outside the gates of Jerusalem. He was the first Martyr. A martyr suffers death or torture rather than deny or change what he believes.

SAINT FRANCIS of Assisi in Italy: Gave up a gay life to go about ragged and hungry, helping the sick and the poor. Everyone loved him and the birds and animals were his friends. His helpers, the Franciscan friars, went barefoot, dressed in rough brown robes.

THE CHRISTIAN CATHOLIC CHURCHES · Roman and Greek

Catholic means universal.
Orthodox means correct, conforming, approved.

GREEK CROSS

LATIN CROSS

THE CHRISTIAN ROMAN CATHOLIC CHURCH—GROWING, BUILDING, ADDING, CHANGING.

ADDED were priests to lead the psalms and prayers, and bishops to oversee the priests, and high bishops—patriarchs —and over all, a Pope.

ADDED to the Sacraments of Baptism, a cleansing with water, and Communion, the Lord's Supper of bread and wine—tokens of the body and blood of Jesus who gave up both—were Confession, an admission of sin, and Penance, prayers and repentance.

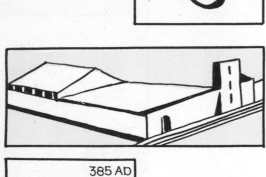

385 AD

ADDED was the Vulgate, the Scriptures collected and translated from Hebrew Old Testament and Greek New Testament writings into Latin by Jerome. It took him twenty-five years. This Vulgate is the official Bible of the Roman Catholic Church.

MANUS DEI

HOLY SPIRIT

HAND OF GOD

ADDED was the Mass, a ritual, with priests and congregation (people assembled to worship) taking part; kneeling, chanting, rising. Added were rosary beads, censers of burning incense, and the crucifix—Christ on the cross.

ADDED was a book, "The City of God," by Augustine, which envisioned a world united in one faith.

312 AD TREFOIL

TRINITY

ADDED were great monasteries, such as Benedict's Monte Cassino, devoted to a simple life and upholding the faith in God and Jesus; and missionary monks of Gregory the Great who took Christianity to England; and convents for women, the nuns.

ADDED were Gregorian chants and choirs.

ADDED was the worship of the Virgin Mary, mother of Jesus, and added was Christmas, the day to celebrate the Christ-child's birth.

ADDING UP AND ADDING UP were more and more people, gathering together for serene, mysterious, uplifting services.

395 AD

PAPAL CROSS

590 AD

HAND OF GOD

GREEK

THE EASTERN ORTHODOX CATHOLIC CHURCH—STANDING FAST.

The early Christian Churches of the East took part in the spread of Christianity in Europe. The Patriarchs of Jerusalem, Antioch, Alexandria, and Constantinople met with the Patriarch of Rome but when he became Pope, head of a Holy Empire, they felt the original idea of Christianity by conviction was being replaced by Christianity by authority.

They had disagreed with many of the new Additions: the worship of the Virgin Mary, compulsory confession, unleavened bread, and the Holy Spirit. Far from the turmoil of lusty Europe, at the eastern end of the Mediterranean, near the homeland of Christianity, they spoke a different language, Greek, and had thoughtful Oriental neighbors. Their viewpoint was very different and they withdrew from the Western Catholic Church alliance.

Their services are conducted as of old: the congregation standing, facing east, with heads uncovered. While their churches are magnificent with rich carpets, marble, candles and paintings, they tolerate no statues, following faithfully the Second Commandment, "Thou shalt not make unto thee any graven image . . ."

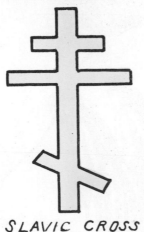

SLAVIC CROSS

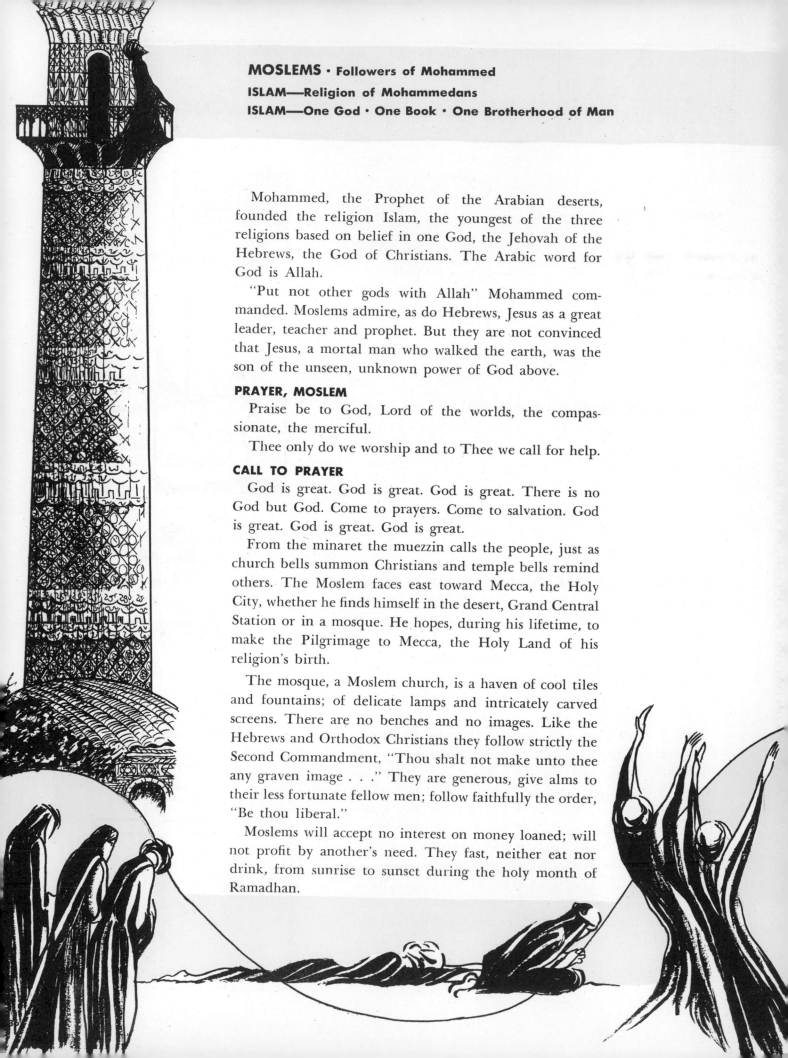

MOSLEMS · Followers of Mohammed
ISLAM—Religion of Mohammedans
ISLAM—One God · One Book · One Brotherhood of Man

Mohammed, the Prophet of the Arabian deserts, founded the religion Islam, the youngest of the three religions based on belief in one God, the Jehovah of the Hebrews, the God of Christians. The Arabic word for God is Allah.

"Put not other gods with Allah" Mohammed commanded. Moslems admire, as do Hebrews, Jesus as a great leader, teacher and prophet. But they are not convinced that Jesus, a mortal man who walked the earth, was the son of the unseen, unknown power of God above.

PRAYER, MOSLEM

Praise be to God, Lord of the worlds, the compassionate, the merciful.

Thee only do we worship and to Thee we call for help.

CALL TO PRAYER

God is great. God is great. God is great. There is no God but God. Come to prayers. Come to salvation. God is great. God is great. God is great.

From the minaret the muezzin calls the people, just as church bells summon Christians and temple bells remind others. The Moslem faces east toward Mecca, the Holy City, whether he finds himself in the desert, Grand Central Station or in a mosque. He hopes, during his lifetime, to make the Pilgrimage to Mecca, the Holy Land of his religion's birth.

The mosque, a Moslem church, is a haven of cool tiles and fountains; of delicate lamps and intricately carved screens. There are no benches and no images. Like the Hebrews and Orthodox Christians they follow strictly the Second Commandment, "Thou shalt not make unto thee any graven image . . ." They are generous, give alms to their less fortunate fellow men; follow faithfully the order, "Be thou liberal."

Moslems will accept no interest on money loaned; will not profit by another's need. They fast, neither eat nor drink, from sunrise to sunset during the holy month of Ramadhan.

THE KORAN

The Koran is the sacred book, the Scriptures, the Bible of Islam. Beautiful designs decorate the pages of graceful writing. In it are the words of God taught by Mohammed. It contains important beliefs, rules for prayers and some parts of the Old Testament. Friday, instead of Saturday or Sunday, is their Holy Day. It promises world brotherhood for every faithful follower, no matter his color, his country, his past sins or beliefs. This youngest religion offers equality—a democracy in heaven for all.

JUDGMENT DAY is also found in the Koran, an event foretold in both Old and New Testaments, described in words of awe and beauty.

"When the sun is folded up and when stars do fall,

"When mountains are moved and the seas rush together and heaven is cleft asunder;

"The Day of Wrath when man must account for his life and deeds."

ASCENSION IN THE NIGHT is the story of Mohammed's journey to Jerusalem and to the gates of heaven on the white, winged steed, Buraq. Guided by the Angel Gabriel, they sped through starlit skies, passed the moon and were greeted by Adam, Moses and Jesus. "Welcome, good son," said Adam. "Welcome, good brother," said Moses. "Welcome, good prophet," said Jesus. On a rock in Jerusalem is a hollow footprint. There, they say, is where Mohammed mounted the magic horse. Jerusalem, as well as Mecca and Medina, has important religious associations for Moslems. The three faiths, those of Hebrews, Christians, Mohammedans, somewhat similar, yet different, claim and want free access to the ancient sun-baked Holy City.

LIFE OF THE PROPHET · Mohammed The Arab

Five hundred and seventy years after Jesus, Mohammed was born in Mecca, oasis town in the wide Arabian deserts. His boyhood as a shepherd gave him many quiet hours for stargazing and dreaming and wondering.

His youth as a camel driver brought him adventure and travel and contacts with caravans from far-off places. He listened around the campfires to the talk about the temple in Jerusalem, about Jehovah and the great prophets; about the churches of Rome, the cross and bells, and Jesus and Christians; about China and India, monks and Buddha and Confucius.

Skillful, handsome and somewhat dreamy, he married a rich widow. Then he traveled less and thought more; thought mostly about one supreme God, Creator and Ruler of All. His belief grew, he convinced his wife and friends, and then he set out as a prophet to teach his countrymen.

In Mecca, in the wall of a square temple, was a sacred stone, the Ka'bah, a meteorite which had fallen long ages before from the heavens. Once a year nomad Arab tribes made long pilgrimages to their holy city. Mohammed talked of God in the market places there. He interrupted the poetry contests; he was jeered and chased and fled to Medina, two hundred miles to the north. This took place in A.D. 622 and is called the Hijrah, the flight.

In Medina the people welcomed him and listened to him. They helped him waylay the Mecca-bound caravans. The Meccans, annoyed, decided to quell the Mohammedans and arrived in a great force outside Medina. They found a trench and a wall had been built around the city; their arrows and spears were useless. Tired from marching and camping, they retreated, grumbling, "Unfair, unheard of . . . ditches and walls."

Mohammed, burning with one ambition, "ONE WORLD WORSHIPING ONE GOD," finally entered Mecca in triumph eight years later. He died soon after, in A.D. 632, master of all Arabia. His friends and followers continued the fight; the tribes united and thousands of fine horsemen swept out to conquer the world for God. "Believe or die!" they insisted. They tried to unite the whole world in one faith.

EVERY MOSLEM IS THE BROTHER OF EVERY OTHER MOSLEM. YOU ARE ON THE SAME EQUALITY.——MOHAMM

ISLAM · Green Flag and Crescent

Green is the color of the religious flag of Moslems. It is said Mohammed unfurled his green turban as a banner while leading his horsemen toward Mecca. The crescent is used on the Turkish national flag and churches probably because Moslems follow the lunar calendar, but maybe because Mohammed was born under a new moon; and when he fled from Mecca to Medina the moon was new; and his visit to heaven was made on a night of the new moon.

Islam, the young, fresh, rousing religion, rode with green flag and scimitar, west into a defeated Jerusalem, a gloomy waiting-for-the-end-of-the-world Christian Europe; into Spain, up into Sicily, to the border of the Holy Roman Empire. Inspired and reckless, Islam rode north through Damascus, east into Baghdad. Bright and eager as they raided, the Moslems picked up as they went mosaics and painting, books and Greek medicine; took along their own astrology, numbers, writing and poetry.

Two of their captive cities forthwith sparkled with beauty and learning; accepted new ideas with enthusiasm. Baghdad became fabulous with marble baths, schools and river pageants. The market places hummed with the trading of beautiful wares; silken carpets, hammered brass and fragile enameled glass. That enchanting book, *The Arabian Nights,* caught the color and brilliance and magic of the times.

Cordova, in sun-dried Spain, became green with orange groves and fountains under the irrigation plan of the invaders. The university and hospital received scholars from great distances. Ideas were discussed; life was gracious and lively at a time when all Europe was held in the dark grip of fear and plagues.

A few hundred years later, Christian Crusaders, bent on recovering the Holy Land, drove the Moslems from some of their strongholds. But to this day there remain in Africa, India, Turkey, China and Arabia, all over the world in fact, great numbers of the faithful. At dawn, at dusk, in sunlight and starlight, they raise their arms to heaven, kneel, bow their heads to the ground in humbleness; pray to God, called Allah.

TRANSLATION:
THERE IS NO GOD BUT GOD AND MOHAMMED IS THE PROPHET OF GOD.

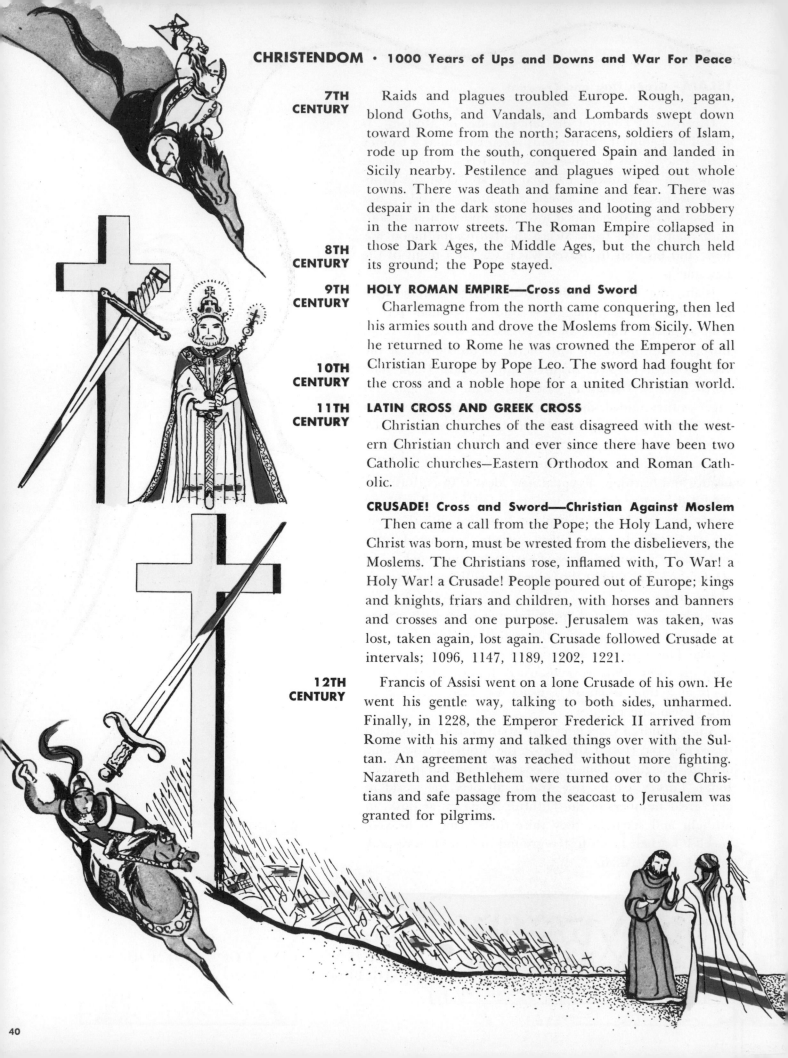

CHRISTENDOM · 1000 Years of Ups and Downs and War For Peace

7TH CENTURY

Raids and plagues troubled Europe. Rough, pagan, blond Goths, and Vandals, and Lombards swept down toward Rome from the north; Saracens, soldiers of Islam, rode up from the south, conquered Spain and landed in Sicily nearby. Pestilence and plagues wiped out whole towns. There was death and famine and fear. There was despair in the dark stone houses and looting and robbery in the narrow streets. The Roman Empire collapsed in those Dark Ages, the Middle Ages, but the church held its ground; the Pope stayed.

8TH CENTURY

9TH CENTURY

HOLY ROMAN EMPIRE—Cross and Sword

Charlemagne from the north came conquering, then led his armies south and drove the Moslems from Sicily. When he returned to Rome he was crowned the Emperor of all Christian Europe by Pope Leo. The sword had fought for the cross and a noble hope for a united Christian world.

10TH CENTURY

11TH CENTURY

LATIN CROSS AND GREEK CROSS

Christian churches of the east disagreed with the western Christian church and ever since there have been two Catholic churches—Eastern Orthodox and Roman Catholic.

CRUSADE! Cross and Sword—Christian Against Moslem

Then came a call from the Pope; the Holy Land, where Christ was born, must be wrested from the disbelievers, the Moslems. The Christians rose, inflamed with, To War! a Holy War! a Crusade! People poured out of Europe; kings and knights, friars and children, with horses and banners and crosses and one purpose. Jerusalem was taken, was lost, taken again, lost again. Crusade followed Crusade at intervals; 1096, 1147, 1189, 1202, 1221.

12TH CENTURY

Francis of Assisi went on a lone Crusade of his own. He went his gentle way, talking to both sides, unharmed. Finally, in 1228, the Emperor Frederick II arrived from Rome with his army and talked things over with the Sultan. An agreement was reached without more fighting. Nazareth and Bethlehem were turned over to the Christians and safe passage from the seacoast to Jerusalem was granted for pilgrims.

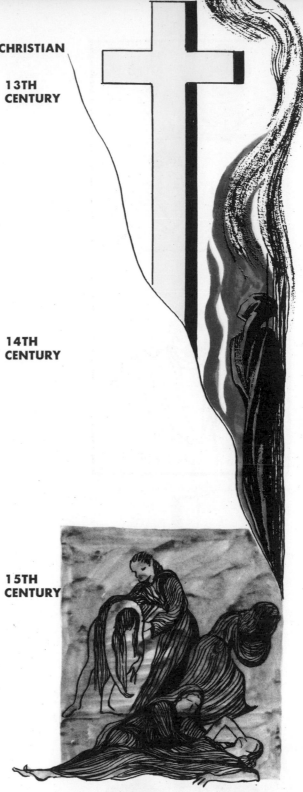

13TH CENTURY

The Roman Catholic church became powerful, rich and strict. There were good popes and bad. Crusaders set out to massacre a Christian group in France, because they held services without priests. Christians were hanged because they did not baptize babies. Christians were burned because they dared criticize clergy and church. People were questioned, tortured and jailed. Innocent people were labeled heretics and witches were tied to the stake. Professors and scientists were under suspicion and many books were forbidden. In Europe the persecution was horrible; in Spain it was gruesome.

14TH CENTURY

The Black Death, a plague, spread over Europe killing thousands, and the black death of cruelty wiped out thousands more. Panic and fear gripped the towns; gates were closed, travel and trading and learning came to a standstill—except in the monasteries. The Jesuit Fathers went on with their simple life devoted to Jesus. Some of them taught, some of them farmed and some spent their lives copying the Bible. Some followed the Explorers to South America, Mexico and Canada; some made their way to China and India.

15TH CENTURY

Then a king defied the Church Law and refused to pay the huge taxes. Other princes questioned the Rule in the name of Religion of the Roman Church.

Churchmen, the Catholic priests, began to protest. Wycliffe, teaching at Oxford, England, argued against the elaborate Mass; wanted a return to the teachings of the Gospel; translated the Latin Bible into English. Rome promptly expelled him, but he held his ground; so many people agreed with him.

Education, reading and thinking and discussion, was on the increase; was no longer confined to the monasteries. The inquiring mind, provided with some tools, inquired.

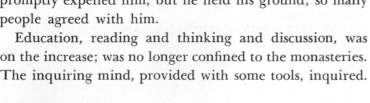

WYCLIFFE

Another priest, in another center of learning, the University of Prague, spoke out against the Church; was tried, and burned at the stake.

A friar in Germany, Martin Luther, outraged by forgiveness-of-sins (Indulgences) for a payment of money, defied the Church. He, too, was tried but the people rose to his defense; so he was not burned. He had given the townspeople the Bible in their own language. They could judge.

Then came Gutenberg's Press, **PRINTING** the Testaments; the Bible in French, in German, in English; lots of Bibles. The puzzled people could buy or borrow and read; could discuss and decide for themselves the important question of the times—whether to follow the Gospels or the Church.

Gutenberg Bible

REFORM! BACK TO THE BOOK. BACK TO THE GOSPEL.

Back to the teachings of Christ, the scholars, the leaders **AND** the people demanded.

16TH CENTURY

THE REFORMATION
CROSS AND BOOK—CATHOLIC AGAINST PROTESTANT

Heretics! Rebels! Disbelievers! answered the Church. North Germans fought South Germans; there were riots in Switzerland. England became Protestant, then Catholic, then Protestant again. Thousands of protesting French Huguenots were massacred in one day. Monasteries were seized, images burned. Europe was torn by religious wars for more than a hundred years.

17TH CENTURY

The terrible wrangling went on, flared up among the reformers themselves. They differed about the *meaning* of the Gospel words; about ways of worship; about kneeling and vestments, one prayer book or another, baptism at birth or later; about colored windows and table or altar. Some thought theaters and sports sinful; others banned music and Communion ceremonies. Dissension was rife, the prisons filled. Trials were held; some got fined and some were hanged. Christians all, but Christians divided.

CROSS AND SCAFFOLD—PROTESTANT AGAINST PROTESTANT

In England the King took over the church. The Church of England (Anglican, Episcopal) was established as *the* Church. In Switzerland the Frenchman, John Calvin, expounded his idea of a *really* Reformed Church. Great numbers of people believed him right. John Knox agreed with his principles and founded the Presbyterian Church of Scotland and Robert Browne organized the Congregational Church in England. Other Calvinist groups called themselves Baptists, Disciples, Reformed, and George Fox gathered together his quiet Friends, the Quakers. Methodists, under the guidance of John Wesley, separated from the Church of England.

And all of them were in trouble. They fought and endured for what they believed the Truth. They moved from England and from France into the calm, but small Low Countries.

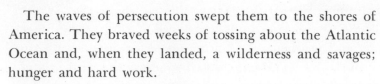

The waves of persecution swept them to the shores of America. They braved weeks of tossing about the Atlantic Ocean and, when they landed, a wilderness and savages; hunger and hard work.

From England in the 1600's came the Puritans to Massachusetts, the Catholics to Maryland, the Quakers to Pennsylvania; from France came the Huguenots who settled in Carolina. With axe and Bible, and courage and faith, they farmed and built cabins and churches; schools and colleges too, for they wanted their children to be able to read the Gospels and new young ministers had to be trained.

Although they had fled to escape intolerance, they themselves had little tolerance for ways of worship not their own. The minister, Roger Williams, and Anne Hutchinson were forced to leave Massachusetts and established a colony in Rhode Island. Public shame in stocks was the punishment for those who broke the strict rules of the church. Witches and heretics who dared differ with the churchmen were hanged by the dozen in Salem, Massachusetts, in 1692.

Fortunately, there was plenty of room in the wide new country. And then, in the 1700's, they found they had to forget their differences and unite against Indian tribes and British armies.

PROTESTANTISM · GROWING

In the United States, the people of the community built, supported and attended the church they wanted. There were no really close ties with the churches of Europe; the ocean was wide, ships and mail slow. They were independent of any government rule and remain so.

Wary of any one-and-only authority, the various groups were individual, single and separate. So individualistic are they still, that there are 250 different kinds of Protestant Churches.

Alongside their churches, schools and colleges were established; they so abhorred ignorance and suppression. A great missionary movement, to spread the ideal Christianity, to help people of other countries, got underway before they were hardly settled, themselves.

Only 400 years old, these Protestant Churches show signs of getting together; uniting for relief work, missionary efforts and religious education. Lately there have been Councils and Conferences, National and International.

In many communities Protestant Minister, Hebrew Rabbi and Catholic Priest sit down at one table, offering in friendly spirit their help and services for the common welfare.

THE MISSIONARIES

A missionary is a person sent out to spread a religious faith.

The list of those who went forth with a message is long. On it are Buddhist monks who crossed the snowy Himalayas to China; the Benedictine monks who started out with Marco Polo; Francis Xavier, the Jesuit priest, who trudged the dusty roads of India, boarded sailing ships and tiny junks, and died on the way to China; Albert Schweitzer, Protestant minister, doctor, professor and musician, who in our own time fights disease and heat and ignorance in the African jungle; the French Peres who set out in canoes from Canadian trading posts, and the Padres from Spain who befriended the Indians of Mexico.

The messages that trickled back from foreign lands are amazing proof of their courage and the strength of their faith.

From Lima, Peru, 1705: "Battled violent headwinds for fifteen days; an error in our maps. . . ."

From St. Thomas, 1732: "He won the hearts of the slaves; the anger of the brutal slave owners. . . ."

From Greenland, 1733: "Smallpox was blamed on them —the missionaries—they tended 2000 ungrateful Eskimos. . . ."

From Melanesia, 1871: "When the Bishop landed, he was murdered. . . ."

From Vancouver, 1875: "Brother Alexis was killed and eaten by an Iroquois Indian. . . ."

From China, 1902: "135 Protestants and 35 Roman Catholics lost their lives in the Boxer Rebellion. . . ."

From the South Seas, 1908: "She, the only white person, worked as teacher, priestess, doctor and friend. . . ."

From Burma, 1940: "I gathered a Gospel team, loaded a mule with medicines and started off. . . ."

From Korea, 1950: "A church was burned; the Evangelist is in the hospital. . . ."

LOWER CALIFORNIA, 1702—a Memoir:

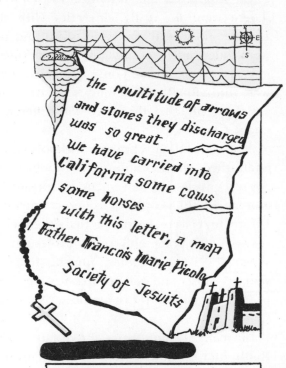

the multitude of arrows and stones they discharged was so great — we have carried into California some cows some horses with this letter, a map

Father Francois Marie Picolo
Society of Jesuits

Brought by faithful hands over land and sea

HERE RESTS

DAVID LIVINGSTONE
1813 - 1873

MISSIONARY, TRAVELLER PHILANTHROPIST

FOR 30 YEARS HIS LIFE WAS SPENT IN UNWEARIED EFFORT TO EVANGELIZE THE NATIVE RACE, TO EXPLORE THE UNDISCOVERED AND ABOLISH THE SLAVE TRADE OF CENTRAL AFRICA

LONDON MISSIONARY SOCIETY

PEKING, CHINA, 1305:   **BURMA, 1943:**

I, alone, in this pilgrimage for 11 years . . . and have built a campanile in which I have put three bells 10 boys I have baptized and taught them Latin letters and our rite . . . and formed a choir

FRANCISCAN FRIAR
John of MONTE CORVINO, ITALY

R̶x̶ We built a hospital . . .
Gordon Seagrave
Baptist

A mission is the post, the station established by the missionary.

They took with them on their mission seeds and telescopes, books and clothes, medicines and tools. Sometimes they took along their wives and children; sometimes, nurses. They healed the sick, took in orphans; taught farming and sanitation as well as prayers. They built hospitals and colleges as well as churches. They tried to change cruel customs. They translated the Bible into Chinese, into Mohican Indian signs; into every strange tongue. They provided the world with dictionaries and maps, reports on strange countries and their customs; they helped record history.

They brought trouble too, unwittingly; measles and influenza germs. They made some mistakes; insisting on shoes where it was healthier to go barefoot. And they were often suspected of trying to overthrow rulers and governments.

Sometimes they were welcomed; sometimes they were ousted. Whether they were successful or failed; whether they were Catholic or Protestant or Buddhist or Moslem —they tried to help their fellow man.

IN PRAISE, IN HONOR, IN GLORY, men struggled to express themselves; at first with rattling gourd, skin drum and hollow reed; with a ram's horn and some twanging strings. Rhythm and chant rose loud and joyous or sweet and sad.

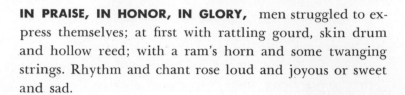

At first he offered something he found: a stone, a pearl, or something he grew—an odd flower, a red root. Then something he made: a string of shells, a clay man, a picture on a palm leaf.

With voice and hands and imagination he created something not for himself, not for his neighbor. For something he believed but could not see, he created beauty of sound and color; pointed steeple, marble temple, the poetry of written words; silvery chimes, shimmering domes and carols on the winter air.

In desert camp and Hebrew temple the Songs of David and the Psalms were wailed. In Asia haunting temple music of flutes and cymbals, strings and drums, called and throbbed, over and over.

6TH CENTURY

Pope Gregory. The Songs of David and the Psalms were chanted in Latin in the early Christian churches (Gregorian Chants). Bells tolled the time for Mass.

7TH CENTURY

The rising swelling sound of the sweet-toned pipe organ suited the religious mood and became part of the somber church services.

10TH CENTURY

A choir of men and boys with good voices rehearsed. Notes for music reading were worked out by Guido d'Arezzo. The choir book was large so all could see; the notes were square.

13TH CENTURY

Traveling troubadours began to sing their news and simple folk tunes. Religious plays and tableaux were performed on movable stages in town squares.

16TH CENTURY—18TH CENTURY

Palestrina led the choir from monotonous song to harmony and part singing. Choirmasters composed majestic music for choir and organ; Handel wrote The Messiah, and Bach worked on his Masses. More music was heard outside the church. Brighter times came and concerts were held, and finally, combining music and acting, operas were presented for the people.

IN PRAISE · The Writers

On clay tablets and skins, on broad leaves of papyrus, on silk, on stone, the artists-with-words wrote the prophecies and laws. On miles of paper the authors and poets recorded the Gospels and teachings, letters and history, confessions and dreams.

IN PRAISE · The Builders

Temples and churches rose higher and higher. The strength and sweat of many men for many years went into their building. Glazed tiles, brick and marble, polished granite and great teak logs were brought from quarry and forest and distant shores by boat, by cart and on the backs of men.

Up went the dome, the spire, bells and stone statues; up went buckets of paint and lunch baskets. Built to last were the houses of worship; paid for with the treasures of Kings and pennies of the poor.

ROMAN CATHOLIC AND CAMPANILE

CATHEDRAL

ADOBE MISSION

PROTESTANT

MOSQUE

HINDU

RUSSIAN ORTHODOX

PYRAMID

BUDDHIST

TORII

PAGODA

SOLOMON'S TEMPLE

IN PRAISE · The Artisans

The talents and patience of many men provided things of great beauty to adorn the interiors of religious meeting places. With knife and chisel, with needle and silk, with bits of glass and chunks of gold they carved and cemented; painted and embroidered.

Eastern Orthodox mosaic, Menorah candlestick, carved wood altar, Mosque enameled glass globe, Roman Catholic jeweled crown and cross, Chinese incense burner, Hebrew Eternal Light lamp, Mosque candlestick, Synagogue velvet curtain.

Arabian prayer rug, Hindu ivory screen, Tallith Hebrew shawl, Catholic Priest's vestment, Chinese carved screen, Christian tapestry, stained glass window.

GOLDEN FIGURES
SILVER SAINTS
BELLS AND BOWLS
CHALICES, CROSSES
CENSERS AND LAMPS
FONTS, FOUNTAINS
ROSARIES, RELIQUARIES
RINGS, PSALTER COVERS

When the turmoil of Christianity's beginnings were over and the resigned waiting for The-End-of-the-World was lifted, the greatest outpouring of magnificent art the world has ever seen took place.

The Orthodox Christians of the early centuries decorated their church in Constantinople with mosaic pictures—tiny colored stones and gold-flecked glass fitted together; 52,000 pieces to one square yard; lovely in color, but stiff and angular.

In the quiet monasteries, monks making Latin and Greek copies of the hand-written Bible, added flowers and gold leaf and tiny pictures to make the pages pretty.

During the Middle Ages, stained-glass windows, painstakingly soldered together, and stiff stone saints became part of the high-pointed Gothic churches. Women plied their needles endlessly making pictures on cloth, tapestries, for castles and cathedrals.

MOSAIC

TAPESTRY

ICON

FRESCO

And then, because there were only a few hand-written books, and because most people could not read, picture stories of the life of Jesus were painted on wet plaster walls by those, born among men since the beginning of time, who must explain with gesture or diagram, clay model or colored sketch—the artists.

They painted on walls of caves, on the walls of churches; they painted a small piece of wood for someone to take home. They added color to wood-carved saints. They mixed varnish and oil with ground colored powders; tried it on cloth, then on canvas; discovered something that would last a long while and could be moved about.

THE PAINTERS AND SCULPTORS

IN PRAISE they painted—not the landscape around them, nor their neighbors—but the glory and wonder of the religion of love and sacrifice and great joy.

Their spirits soared, and they put down for mankind the mystery and vision of hope for the world: the Annunciation, the Nativity, the Last Supper, the Crucifixion, the Ascension, the Apostles and Madonnas; the Creation, Adam and Eve, the Prophets, Heaven and Hell as described in the Testaments and as imagined.

The story of Christ glowed from the ceilings and walls of churches and schools. It became part of everyday living: Virgin and Child over doorways and in homes, Biblical figures on great bronze gates.

The artists created, the emperors encouraged and the people adored. They spent hours, days, a lifetime, on magnificent statues and exquisite chapels. Inspired, they, in their own way, using their special talents, worked to carry the message of Jesus to their neighbors and beyond—to those not yet born; the children, grandchildren, and great-great-great-grandchildren of the future.

NOWADAYS

In 1791 the Bill of Rights was added to the Constitution of the new United States of America. Article I reads,

CONGRESS SHALL MAKE NO LAW RESPECTING ESTAB-LISHMENT OF RELIGION, OR PROHIBITING FREE EXERCISE THEREOF: . . .

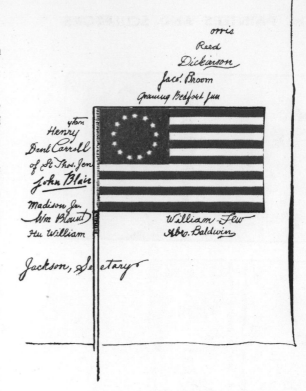

And that is the way it has been ever since. The bells of Catholic and Protestant churches ring out together on a Sunday morning. People are free to hold Revival Meetings, Sunday School parades, and Saints' Day processions. In the West, Indians gather to perform their ceremonial Sun Dance, and on city streets Chinese celebrate a religious holiday with firecrackers and paper dragons. Americans respect the spires and crosses and stars and domes of each other's churches and take for granted the rights of all to choose their way of worship.

Nowadays, there is more tolerance and respect for the beliefs and ways of worship of others; more efforts directed toward understanding and getting together.

There are still unhappy outbreaks, rioting, imprisonment, evacuation and death due to religious differences. There are still remnants of old superstitions, Voodoo, in Africa, Australia, the West Indies and in the South.

Not yet is there Peace on Earth, Good Will toward Men. Man, having accomplished scientific miracles, pauses. He hesitates, he looks for guidance, he turns to God. He, like the earliest man, ponders the Mystery.

The Four Freedoms
January 6, 1941

In the future days . . . we look forward for a world founded upon four essential, human freedoms. . . . The second is freedom of every person to worship God in his own way—everywhere in the world.

—President Franklin Delano Roosevelt

United Nations Charter
October 24, 1945

Article I.

. . . to achieve . . . respect for human rights and for the fundamental freedoms for all without distinction as to race, sex, language or religion:

Signed by 59 nations in 1950 after World War II

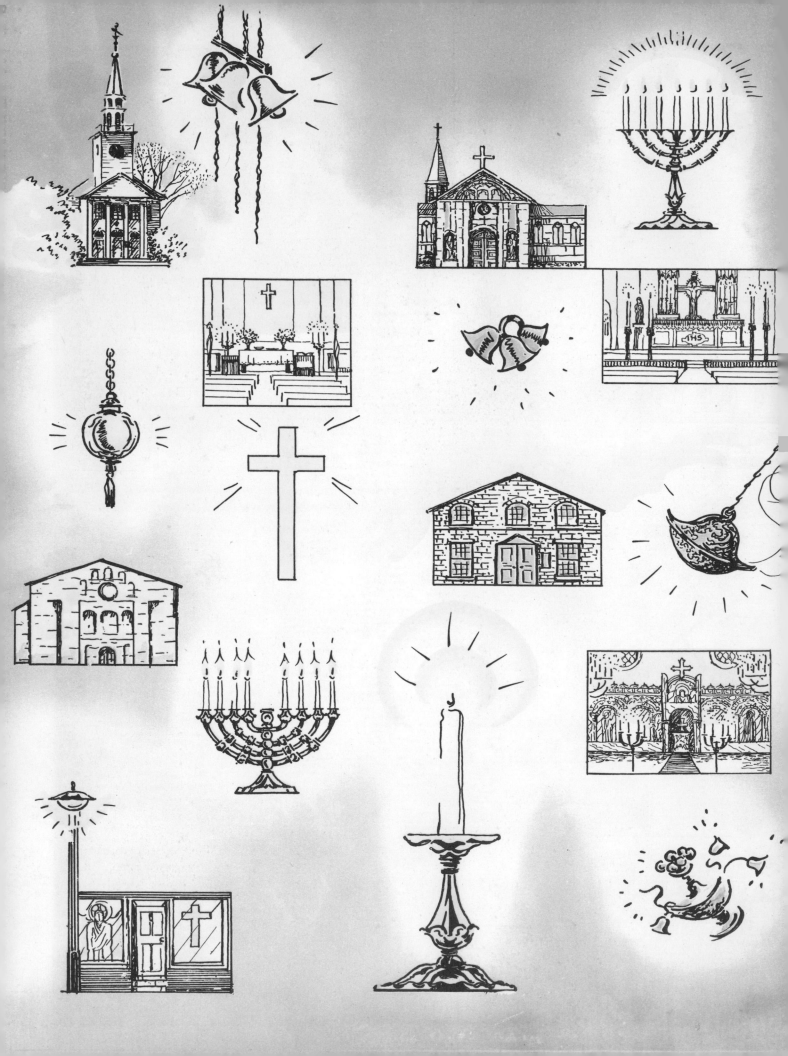